50 Years of Nice
Marriage Stories

June Walters

ISBN: 1505596637
ISBN 13: 9781505596632
Library of Congress Control Number: 2014922390
CreateSpace Independent Publishing Platform
North Charleston, South Carolina

Dedication

To my parents, Harry and Mary Weber
To Aunt Rose and Uncle Frank
To Aunt Frances and Uncle George
And to my sister Dottie and her husband, Ed
All had happy marriages of fifty or more years.

Acknowledgments

Cover Photo by Samuel John
(https://www.flickr.com/photos/SamuelJohn/5377978827/)
Used under Creative Commons License.
Thank you to my daughter, Catherine Salomon Sweet and
to granddaughter Christine Sweet who gave me guidance.
Thank you to the people I interviewed.
Thank you to my husband, Gene Walters, and to Barbara
of CreateSpace for editing.

All interviewed people have given me permission for
publication.

50 Years of Nice

Marriage Stories

Contents

Preface

Fifty Years of Nice

I take you to be my wedded wife to have and to hold in sickness and in health, in good times and in bad, and in joy as well as in sorrow.

In the presence of God and our friends I take thee to be my husband and promise to be a loving and faithful wife so long as we both shall live.

To honor and respect you, to laugh and cry with you, and to cherish you for as long as we both shall live.

Your people will be my people, and your God will be my God.

With this ring I thee wed.

From this day forward, I promise…to share…

For better or worse, richer or poorer; to love, to cherish from this day forward.

Marriage is a good thing. It is an honorable convention, something to value, role model, enjoy, take great pride in, grow in, and have fun in. It is wonderful to visit with couples who have lived together for five or more decades, as there is something so pleasant about being around them. I think it is the referencing they do of each other, the all-knowing of the other, and the memories they evoke in each other. Whatever it is, it shows.

Marriages that have endured for forty, fifty, and more years are in the minority in our country. About 5 percent of all current marriages have existed for fifty or more years. To keep that in perspective, being married for more than fifty years would probably mean the couples are in their seventies, eighties, and beyond. In the last census, there were about 13 million people in the age range of seventy-five to eighty-four; 7½ million were women. Fifteen percent of Americans are over sixty-five years of age, and that percentage is increasing. Viewing statistics like these, it is clear that even though the number of people growing older is increasing, because they are living longer, the number of long-lasting marriages is not.

Doing simple computer research, reading magazines and newspapers, and just listening to TV and people in general tells us that most marriages today have a hard time reaching double digits. Whether it is around the second year, the fourth year, or the seventh year, aggravations seem to show up in certain years. With children of divorced parents growing up and marrying, there's a whole group who perhaps didn't get to see disagreements settled in compromise or at least peacefully. Rather the outcome might have been "This isn't working; I'm outta here."

In the light of all this, how come some marriages last until their golden anniversaries and beyond? What have those couples done and done well enough to stay happy? Can we learn from them?

What about conflict resolution? Established in Germany in the 1920s, conflict resolution was brought to the States in the 1930's. This form of negotiating wasn't even thought of as applicable to marriages mid-20th century, rather they were guidelines and processes for companies, for labor unions and for countries. Eventually that process evolved into being applicable as counseling and therapeutic techniques for people in marriage encounters, couple's counseling, individual therapy and more. This was not at all the first thought by most of the couples married for fifty of more years. This is not to say some did not go to counseling and some found it useful, some, not. So, when there were disagreements, what were the most effective ways of resolution used by the successfully married people? They have said over and over...communication; talk about everything... and compromise. As you read the stories it is evident that most individuals knew themselves pretty well, understood the separate but connected roles as husband and wife and each took responsibility seriously. Much of the time when an issue arose which was debatable or arguable or stirred up differing emotions, it seemed that because each spouse's position within the marriage was well defined, the issue could be resolved without much fanfare, certainly not with thoughts of leaving each other.

Consider this perhaps simple analogy.

When I was young, my Dad was going to paint my bedroom. I wanted to help and couldn't wait to just get in there with the paintbrush and go at the walls. "Wait, a lot to do before we open that paint!" said he. "Lay some paint cloths on the floor, clean the walls, fill in the holes with putty, sand those areas, tape around the windows, take off the floor moldings carefully, prime the walls, open the paint can carefully, stir it really well, and then we're ready to begin to paint."   So, the analogy being, preparation prior to the event works.

A few couples acknowledged they just never argued, truly. It could be attributed to total love and kindness for the partner. Jean Krowka said to ask yourself before marriage would you do absolutely anything for this man? If the answer is not yes, perhaps marriage should be delayed.

The couples interviewed did not spend money foolishly in their early years when for most, money was 'tight'. If they didn't have it, they didn't spend it. This helps, ahead of time, to avoid many arguments couples can have relative to finances. The same goal of what to do with (or without) money and the same living style of 'not keeping up with the Joneses' by both spouses absolutely contributes to more peaceful times.

When the interviewed couples were asked about marriages lasting or breaking up, these are some of the insights offered.

It all takes time. Talking about what you do *with* money and what you do *without* money is important to stay in a marriage. Sometimes marriages *break* when financial problems beset couples. Sometimes couples are not financially on the same page, or one or neither partner has concepts to express. Although possibly time-consuming, discussions before and during marriage are needed.

Immaturity seems to play a large part in doomed marriages. That would account for a "me first" attitude or even the belief that "let's have kids and it'll help our marriage."

It works better when each person has grown up before marriage and knows himself or herself pretty well.

It certainly takes more than starry eyes and nights to hold a marriage together. There are hundreds of books on staying appealing, particularly relative to the sexual life of a marriage. Magazines tell women how to be more sensual and what men *really* like in bed, and advice columns query, "Can this marriage be saved?" Marriages based on only physical attraction or sexual needs don't seem to make it. There needs to be a great deal more going on in the relationship. The emotional and behavioral maturity level of each person means something. One needs to be fully in charge of oneself. Know who you are and how to get along with others, preferably before marriage.

More than one husband who was interviewed had lost a job or had to accept early retirement. More than one wife didn't follow her training/degree or become fulfilled in her career early in the marriage. Yet neither of these situations were marriage breakers nor even marriage "disturbers." I believe it is because there had been either consciously or subtly established standards and goals for their marriages, and difficult situations were faced as a team.

Becoming and staying friends, and having respect and concern for the other are paramount. The interviewed couples listened to each other, they looked at one another when they spoke, and they talked positively about their mates.

"Bev gets along really well with people."

"Tony always stood by me relative to the children."

"Bob is there for me...always."

"Ed is so straight and fair."

"I thought Sue was the prettiest girl there, and we had fun together."

"I thought Joe was really good-looking, and he and my family got along so well."

"I would not be here were it not for Maria."

"I respect Stu."

"I respect Eileen."

"I respect Peg."

"I respect Sue."

"I respect Jean."

"I became head over heels in love with Ruth."

"I thought Hilda was pretty and wanted to ask her out."

"I respect him."

"Eileen and I had a beginning bond between us."

"Elaine and I discussed children and money before marriage."

"Ray and I planned our recreational activities to be with the kids."

Then there are the skills of negotiation and problem solving.

"Pat and I think alike on the important issues."

"Sal and I talk about everything."

"Compromise," said Sue, Joan, Al, and a few others.

"Ruth and I had the same goals, and we did talk about the future a lot."

"We just never argued because Tony and I had defined our roles pretty well."

"Ed and I take our responsibilities and appreciate the family unit."

"Communication is important," said most.

"Bob and I seemed always to be on the same page."

"Phil's sense of humor saved us more than once."

"Ray and I discuss everything."

"When we make decisions, I put Ed first, and I know he thinks of me first."

Many said marriage was work. As Bob Gluck said, "Don't give up." Nancy and Sal Franco said, "Stick it out!" Most also said the occasional argument was brief and couples moved on.

As one might surmise, most all were married in the 1950s and 1960s and lived in similar economic times. No one in our interviewed group was in the upper-upper economic class, and no one was in the lower economic class. There were similarities in that purchasing and saving was not as difficult as it is today, and many didn't start out having a credit card. Buying a home was assumed and accomplished without the harrowing aspects of ARM interest rates and home equity over borrowing.

More than one courting gentleman saved dollars and bought his first car. When Ralph Edwards was dating Ruth, he thought, "I knew I had to get a set of wheels. I had saved some money while I was in the service and had had my parents hang on to it for me. So I did just that, I bought a car." Cars and homes were not given as gifts from families; rather they were saved for and purchased by the couples when they met their saving money goal. They did things for themselves and saved together. Financial goals were the same for all: save, have a little extra to spend maybe, buy a home, improve that home, and save for the family. Everyone worked on their homes, from Joe Bruschetti finishing off the upstairs of a Cape Cod, and Carl and Pat Foucht planting future Christmas trees, to Chuck Van Velson improving his home and yard, and Al Russell completing his finished basement. No one hired home-improvement folks; they did it themselves. They enjoyed doing it themselves.

During the 1940s through the 1960s, social mores pretty much defined the preferred way to care for children. That was not to attend day care, but rather be cared for at home by Mom or a close relative or friend. One mom did return to teaching, and her children were cared for by a family friend, a stay-at-home mom. To have children cared for by strangers in a strange setting, and from early hours in the morning to the supper hour, just wasn't a consideration. Joe and Sue Bruschetti said, "Everything was for the kids." Maria and Ed Alsfeld agreed, "Everything throughout our whole marriage was for our children." Ruth and Ralph Edwards said, "We had closely knit families." Bea Schantz said that she and Dick were family focused. Jean and Ed Krowka appreciated their family unit. Carl and Pat Foucht said, "We designed activities to include all the family," and Sal and Nancy Franco said they pulled together, especially with family. When you read these stories, this practice of family love, family involvement, and family first will be evident over and over.

That era was also the beginning of questioning some family/religious ethics. Some couples, such as Joan and Chuck Van Velson and Bea and Dick Schantz, were raised in different religions, and their parents wanted them to marry within the faith. When they did marry, neither couple's entire families attended the service or the reception. It was an issue for the parents. But, in both instances, each couple joined in one faith and raised their children in that faith, and the extended families came to accept this. Age was also an issue with some of the parents. Chuck was several years older than Joan, and her parents tried to make her see that she shouldn't be dating him. Sue Bruschetti delayed telling her parents that Joe was a few years older. Happily, they all did marry, and it worked out just fine. But, again, it had been an issue. Stu and Bev Silvester decided that Stu would attend seminary after they were married, which meant not having a home built for a while. Bev's family frowned upon Stu returning to college as a family man. That idea was an issue back in the day. Today there are different issues, but the extended family's view doesn't seem to matter or be much of an influence. Sue and Joe were totally immersed in Sue's family, and their views and influence absolutely did make a difference, a positive influence. Family values, family activities, and family closeness attributed to their fifty-plus years of marriage. Jane and Phil Lehrbach lived with his family for a while, and it benefited the couple and Phil's parents. Hilda and Al Russell had little blood family but filled their lives with twenty to thirty people who had a similar German heritage, and they became close like family. Each couple interviewed has a respect for most of their extended families or family-like people and allow them to be a favorable influence.

It also seems as if most interviewed wives did find a second career…after a while. So wasn't it grand having been a woman in those earlier years? She could raise children at home and later be able to work outside of the home too. How nice is that: the best of both worlds.

Most couples in so many words thought that having your own space, your own activity, and maybe your own set of a few friends was important, in addition to what you did as a couple.

The intention of this book is twofold. One, in the grand scheme of living, there seems to be a fair amount of downer stuff, bad things happening. Wouldn't it be just plain *nice* to read about something *nice*, with no strings attached, no fear or disturbance, no quiz at the end, and no grand summaries to assess? The second reason is that maybe, just maybe, there are people about to get married, or who will someday get married, or are married and having some difficulties, for whom reading about healthy and successful marriages could make a difference.

Being of the age I am, and most of my friends in relatively the same senior age bracket, I am fortunate to know many couples who have been married for fifty or more years. Ed and Maria Alsfeld are the most recent of my friends, we having met through our tennis club. All of the others have been friends of mine for a long time as we have met either in New York State or Florida.

I asked my friends if they would tell me their stories, if I could write them down, and if I could publish them. A date was made to talk about their marriage. That led to an hour or so of sitting down with individual couples and, in two instances, the widows who had had over fifty years of marriage. There were no particular questions posed. They spoke, and I took down everything they said.

"Tell me about your marriage," I said. And they did.

Prior to our interview, some had planned who would speak first, and others just looked at each other and said, "You start." Most of the interviewed people told me how they met and then told their marriage story chronologically.

Some spoke candidly about occasional difficulties within a marriage, children who had been the difficulty of the marriage at times, and other specific problems. I opted to leave those specifics on the kitchen table, which is where most of the interviews took place. What I did write about, relative to those situations, was how the couple was able to cope and stay in a positive relationship. The only two questions I did ask were: "Why do you think you've been married for all these years?" and "And why do you think other marriages don't make it?" While it may seem that the responses to the first question would be just the reverse of the responses to the second, they rarely were.

No couple needed prompting. The exceptions were my two widowed women friends. Although each had agreed to be interviewed, I believe they may have found retelling their memories, talking for a half hour or more, a bit more difficult. I felt badly when Bea recalled the one major tragedy in her and Dick's life: the premature death of their thirty-one-year-old son, Kevin. It was part of the marriage story, but to go it alone in the retelling was sad. On the other hand, her husband was a dynamo, and they had a fun marriage, so we continued in the process.

At the end of the interviews, most of the husbands remarked that they had enjoyed it, surprisingly, as some of the men were not quite as enthusiastic when first asked. This has been a feel-good experience for me, as I am the beneficiary of these wonderful stories. Even before the hour or so of talking was done, there was a thread running through the tapestry of their marriage, which was one of the major clues to what makes a good, long, and happy marriage. I didn't know it was going to happen that way. Before I actually approached the fourteen couples, I had shared my story idea with a friend, a published author. She suggested that it might be a good idea to prepare a questionnaire for the couples to look over prior to our meeting. I considered it, but without a structure, I thought each couple's own style and personalities would show through better. The process I used had no particular guidelines, and it resulted with fourteen different styles of rhetoric. Nice!

My original criterion was a *nice* marriage of fifty or more years, period. However, I came to know the Franco's well and to appreciate their particular story. They are not at the fifty-year mark yet, but I wanted to include them because I felt *nice* being around them. Each had a prior marriage, and their spouses had died young. Each had three children to raise by themselves. When they found each other, they married, raised six children, and then had a child of their own. I knew their story should be included.

There was something different about each couple that seemed to contribute to keeping the marriage solid and long. Eileen and Bob had a busy business life in common, which kept them together around the clock sometimes, as they always did whatever was in front of them, and much was in front of them. They did what they had to do in order to live. Ed and Maria learned together how to raise a cow, a goat, and more. And in Stu and Bev's lives, God's plan was evident all the time; they simply trusted him and let him show the way, even when it seemed to be a tough road. Jean and Ed, Peg and Tony, Carl and Pat, and Joan and Chuck all found activities and the sports world as they approached, in some cases, new sports and new pastimes together. They played together. Ruth and Ralph, Bea and

Dick, and Jane and Phil found recreational pastimes together, such as cards or dancing. Hilda and Al entertained and socialized with a close group of friends who were like family. Ray and Elaine and I are grandparents to the same now-adults, so their values as a married couple were not only known to me personally but also respected. Sue and Joe, as well as Sal and Nancy, stayed closely tied to large, extended families.

Each partner seemed to be in touch with his or her own individual character and definitely had his or her own morals, ethics, and standards pretty well established. So each individual became a healthy part of the whole.

All couples used similar words relative to why they thought they had achieved a nice long marriage. That should be no surprise as these skills are also key in any healthy relationship:

- Communication
- Sense of humor
- Sensitivity
- Endurance
- Tolerance of one another's faults

At the completion of each story, there are specifics as to why the marriage has been what it is and why, perhaps, they think some marriages end in divorce.

When I first asked a couple if I could interview them about their marriage, some said yes right away, some were hesitant, some thought it would be fun, and some said, "Oh, what would we say?" Some declined, and there are still couples who planned to be involved, but time constraints and distance got in the way.

I explained what my incentive was: their marriages looked *nice* to me and I wanted to write something to make people feel *nice*, like author Jan Karon's writings do for me. These stories might be read by people prior to getting married or people having difficulties in their early marriage years. Perhaps these fourteen couples' stories will enlighten them. They talked about and exhibited winning traits. So it seems certain that these traits could be the groundwork for success for others' marriages.

I am grateful for the time my friends gave me.

This is the process I used. With a blank document on my laptop screen, I asked them to start talking, and I just typed every word they said, sometimes encouraging a little deeper detail. After an hour or so, we could feel ourselves winding down. They went home, or in the case of a few, I went home and put my notes about them into some sort of a story. When I had a pretty good draft completed, I gave it to the couple, asking for any kind of editing, deletions, additions, rearrangements, or whatever they wished. After this stage was completed, I incorporated their notes into a finished essay and sent it again to the couples.

When I was writing the first draft, I also did some research of perhaps their hometown, their college, their jobs, and certainly specific years and locations. I love putting the couple against a historical timeline. Not any of the participants knew all of the others in the book, but everyone knew a few. Each signed a permission form allowing me to publish their stories. One of my granddaughters and her mom (my daughter) came up with the book cover. Encouragement came from family and friends.

I loved doing this. I wish I could have interviewed and written about every couple I know, as they each are walking stories with something to offer.

Thank you, my friends, from the bottom of my heart and ink cartridges. Let's hope this saves someone's marriage. On to sixty.

Marriage Stories

Jean and Ed Krowka
June 4, 1958

Learn from each other.

"Five foot two, eyes of blue, but oh what those five foot could do…" This is a "Jeannie song." Only, for her, it would be "Five foot four, eyes of brown…but oh what those five foot could do…Never had another beau" except Edmund Krowka.

More than likely you'll see Jean in a stunning outfit with heels a few inches high, a great necklace, pretty finger rings, and just the right amount of makeup. Her posture is ramrod straight, and she's just all femininity and grace. Her guy is her equal, although Jean says, "We are opposites in some things. He is very cool, calm, and collected. I can blow up quickly. But they say opposites attract. I wish I had his patience," she said, "I really do."

When the two of them are on the dance floor or the tennis courts, or at a supper, or sitting across from me any-place, they are a knockout couple. Ed, nearly six foot, has a physique that rivals the fifty-year olds in the neighbor-hood. And a lot of guys his age have shoulders that seem to slump and disappear. Not his broad ones. What I like most about this couple's physical appearance is the crinkly lines at the sides of their eyes. You know what that's from: smil-ing, laughing, and in general having a positive, pleasant look on their faces.

"We celebrated our fiftieth wedding anniversary a cou-ple of years ago and took a Caribbean cruise. We were in the lounge one evening, and there were about seven or eight young folks there. We mingled with them and told them how long we were married. They couldn't believe it and asked, 'How did you last so long? How did you do it?' That hit me right between the eyes, the fact that they were so amazed.

"You need a sense of humor and big-time communica-tion," he added.

"There was a time that I didn't think it would happen, a marriage that is. He took his sweet time, like five and half years," Jean said and laughed. "But before Ed and I were married, we got all of that dating out of our system, for all of those over five years. Then we settled down and took on our responsibilities."

"I do recall one funny experience we had before we set-tled down, and that was at Port Everglades," said Ed. "We decided to go fishing, picnic, and also enjoy each other. So we figured out how to have the fishing line working with-out our actually having to hold it. There was a tree near the shore, and both of us jumped up and dangled from a branch, testing the strength. It was going to work. So we wound the clothesline around the branch, extended it, and coiled it on the seawall. Then we didn't have to tend it. Well, something else did tend it, and all of a sudden, the branch snapped off and was pulled lickety-split into the water. It had to be a huge fish, maybe a shark, that got away."

1952

President Harry S. Truman served out his term and decided not to run again. General Dwight D. Eisenhower defeated Adlai Stevenson, becoming the thirty-fourth president of our forty-eight states. Both men were well known and admired, but "Ike" was revered for his role in the military, serving and leading us to a World War II victory. It was in the middle of the Korean War, which would last a dreadful three years and settle a year later, forever dividing that little country into north and south. Israel became a state and the cold war continued. Elizabeth II, still in her twenties, became queen upon her father's, George VI, death. Polio had been and was an epidemic, paralyzing thousands of children and killing over three thousand. Jonas Salk invented a polio vaccine, which was to become widely used, though not until a few years later.

Gasoline was twenty cents a gallon; hamburger, fifty cents a pound; peanut butter, twenty-nine cents; and for three fifty you could buy fashion gloves *and* a pocketbook. Nylons, a daily must, were two pairs for a dollar. Women's styles included full and flouncy skirts and form-fitting sheaths, all a tad below the knee and feminine. There was a kind of standard outfit that almost everyone wore for business, going out socially, running errands, house or yard work, and maternity. You had to wear the proper clothing for the proper chore. And it seems Jean does that still. When she and Ed go out, people's heads turn; on the tennis courts, her little skirts are perfectly color coordinated with hat and shirt.

The average salary was $3,850. For half of that, you could buy a car, and for double that, a starter home. Roll-on deodorant and the *Today* show, starring Dave Garroway, were introduced. A variety of electronics were available: radio-phono consoles, hi-fis with radios, consoles with record players that would hold ten records, and AM-FM radios. A twenty-one-inch Silvertone Console TV sold for $339.

Baseball, long America's pastime, continued to be the major sport with the Yankees, Dodgers, and Giants, all New York teams, commanding the most fans. But with the advent and popularity of TV, football, boxing, and ice hockey became prominent and popular. Ice hockey fans saw the Zamboni and goalies wearing face masks. Contrary to current news, the Cleveland Browns were right up there, winning the NFL Championship three times.

And that leads us to the Tommies football team, the Cigar Bowl, the Detroit Lions, and Ed.

Ed was born in 1927, in Chicago, Illinois, to Michael and Josephine Krowka. Mike and Josephine had come from Poland, Galicia, or Austria-Hungary, as it was known then. They arrived at Ellis Island in the first decade of the 1900s and met in Chicago. Their marriage document says, "Michael Krowka, age 21, married Jozefa Warrenda, age 19, on June 25, 1912."

"Dad came with his brothers, Joe, John, and Tom, and almost immediately started up a business. Dad started a bar and then went into the wholesale rose business in Chicago. Tom was a florist, wholesale and retail, John did wholesale rose growing, and Joe went into the mushroom business. All self-reliant."

Ed grew up near Chicago in a large family. At one time his uncle and aunt lived with them, and then there was his sister, Bertha, and brothers Teddy, Edwin ("Moe"), and Michael.

"My parents had a baby, Ed, who died at birth, and then my brother Teddy died on the basketball court when he was only eighteen years old. He died of a heart problem. That was hard to take." Basically, though, he had a fine childhood. "My parents were good parents."

The College of St. Thomas was a private, Catholic liberal arts school in St. Paul, Minnesota, where Ed "Fingers" Krowka was the star quarterback. He could throw a ball three quarters down the field and was MVP, and is now in their Hall of Fame for athletics.

"Krowka Makes Grid History" ran a newspaper headline, and another ran a picture of the Polish-bred guy dropping his Polish sausage when he heard the news that their team was going to the Cigar Bowl. The game was played at Phillips Field in Tampa, Florida, on New Year's Day 1949 and ended at a thirteen-thirteen tie. Next, Ed became a drafted quarterback for the Detroit Lions.

"Wow, a dream. I was going to play football for the Detroit Lions. However, it ended a brief three days later when the medical team found a heart murmur, and they felt I shouldn't play. I had played football all through high school and college, but the Lions' pros said no. They brought up the liability factor. All three doctors agreed and gave me the pink slip. It was heartbreaking. I had to go to a doctor for depression, wound up in the hospital, had shock treatments with a strap around the head for which you're zonked out, and afterward had no anxieties, a pure beautiful feeling, for a half hour or so. I finally got out of it and came back to normalcy."

A state or so west, in 1929, Jean was born.

Hibbing, Minnesota, was known as "The Town That Moved," "Grand Canyon of the North," and "Iron Capital of the World." The largest open-pit iron mine around was located in northern Minnesota. When iron ore was discovered under the original town, back in 1893, it was decided to move the town. So they did, building by building, to a site two miles south over five years. Hence, the nicknames for the town.

It was there that Jean was born in 1929. "My family life was different from Ed's. My mom's mother, my grandmother Sellars, raised me, and my sister stayed with our father's mother. Because of her religious influence, my grandmother kept me under her thumb. I think back to what she did for me; I thank God every day that she was there doing for me. Being brought up that way made me want a family unit badly."

Jean talked about her grandmother Mancuso in Kittsville. "She had twenty-one children; fourteen of them lived. We visited Grandma and Grandpa Mancuso in Minnesota. They had no flooring, just dirt, and the goats and other animals came into the house. My grandma didn't speak much English, and Grandpa was teaching me Italian. I can still say numbers in Italian!"

A Little Bit of History

In the middle of the nineteenth century, in agrarian America, farm machinery inventions were important, and when the reaper was invented by Cyrus McCormick, his harvesting machine company was founded and became successful. Eventually, with other agricultural machinery, the company expanded and became known as International Harvester, employing many in Melrose Park, Illinois. Today it exists as primarily an automotive company called Navistar International. Melrose Park, a suburb of Chicago, is a village that used to have a large Italian American population, but now the majority is Mexican American, and it is still an industrial town.

So it was that in 1952, both Jean and Ed worked at International Harvester.

"When I first saw Ed at work, I thought he was married. I would have no chance to date a guy so good-looking. He was so handsome. I was trying so hard to meet him. I worked on the mezzanine floor where the coffee break area was," said Jean, "and Ed and another fellow, Cunningham, would come up for a break."

"Well," Ed said, "I noticed this little chick and told Cunningham I wanted to date her, and Cunningham told Jean that. It still took me a while to ask her out."

Jean recalled, "We saw each other around the cafeteria where a bunch of us would go for lunch. Ed would be there or walk by with a couple of guys. I'd always look at him when he went by. One day I was taking some TD tractor blueprints to distribute to different departments. Ed's department was in the basement, and when I went downstairs,

Ed was coming toward me. I was going in the opposite direction, and he walked right by me. That surprised me. Was this the guy I wanted to meet? It took Ed three or four months before he asked me out for a date."

"But," explained Ed, "I thought you were so good-looking that I didn't have a chance."

"I don't know why he took so long," Jean said. "I didn't have a phone, so I asked my neighbor if I could give Ed their phone number. They said yes, and I gave Ed the phone number as he had finally asked. He called, and from then on we were steady partners."

"Our first date was a Saturday night," said Ed, "and we went to Club Hollywood, a beautiful club with a great dance band. We had our picture taken."

"That picture is on our wall at home."

"(We) danced together, sat at the bar..."

"We sat at a table..."

"All very enjoyable," Ed said. "There was a place, an inn called Point Comfort, and every weekend we'd go there. All night you're dancing, drinking, meeting people, and talking to the bartender. The first time we were there, just for fun we asked how much the rooms were. They thought we were poor, and they gave us a break in the price. We were only asking.

"It was a rickety old resort on Fox Lake about thirty miles northwest of Chicago. We did a lot of fishing there, too."

Jean and Ed dated steadily and talked about heading out of town. Jean didn't have such a great home life, and Ed was ready to move out of his family home. They each had saved some money, so in 1956, they moved to Florida. Ed got a place of his own, and Jean had an apartment with another girlfriend.

"Well," said Jean, "we dated and dated and dated, and then it was five and half years that we dated. I loved this man so much…I mean it…but I was getting tired of waiting. I thought, 'If he's not going to make up his mind, I need to find out if we're going to get married. He better let me know.' We were in Walgreens and Ed said, 'It's about time we stayed together and got married.' And I asked, 'Is that a proposal?' I supposed it was. I told him yes and that we ought to call his parents.

"Ed gave me an engagement ring in April, and in June 1958, we were married. His parents and brother came down for the occasion and actually ended up with us on our honeymoon. Ed's father gave me away, and we came in from each side of the church instead of the aisle. I made my own dress."

"It was beautiful," said Ed.

"And I bought Ed a new suit for Christmas, a nice off-white, and that's what he wore. Except something happened on the way to the church. Something happened with the zipper. Ed's mother, his father, and he all had to work on that zipper to make it work. Last-minute stuff.

"And Ed's wedding ring had to be so big that it was a special order. It arrived just in time for the wedding.

"My dress was mid calf length, white silk material, plain, and simple with a little train that reached to the floor. I wore four-inch high heels. The lady who did my hair didn't charge me because it was a gift for my wedding. I had a simple bouquet.

"I had stayed at another place just prior to our wedding so his parents could stay in my apartment. We were married by a young, twenty-four-year-old priest who had been ordained in Ireland and came here to St. Anthony's. We had about ten people; Ed's landlady came, too. Pa, Ed's father, took us to the Sea Horse Hotel—it's no longer there—on the beach for breakfast. It was very nice. Ed's parents paid for almost everything. We also had a little reception in our apartment."

Ed added, "This young priest gave Jean instruction in the Catholic religion for about two weeks. She converted. He later baptized both of our kids, and we retook our vows on our twenty-fifth wedding anniversary. We were supposed to do it for our fiftieth, too, but the priest became ill."

"We went to the Keys for our honeymoon," said Jean. "I think that's why our son loves it and works there now. Ed's parents and brother came to Marathon, too, for our honeymoon. Ed's dad loved fishing."

"Well, the next day," Ed tells the story, "we were supposed to go fishing together on a bottom boat. My dad was all set. The first day of our honeymoon, he came knocking on our door with a bag of groceries to take on the boat. The water was very wavy; I had been in the navy so maybe had sea legs. Dad and my brother got seasick. We got on shore, and Jean laughed and laughed. She and my mom ribbed them a lot, especially my mom."

"We stayed at the Keys for about four days, and then Ed moved into my apartment," Jean said. "The girl I was sharing with moved back to her parents' place. Our apartment had three large rooms, and we paid seventy-five dollars a month for it. We lived on Seventh Avenue in Fort Lauderdale. I worked at Beale's, and Ed worked at the Fort Lauderdale post office." That was 1958.

1958

Dwight D. Eisenhower was still president; Democrat Leroy Collins was governor of Florida. The Vietnam War began, and a year later, Alaska and Hawaii became the forty-ninth and fifth states. A recession was leveling off, but unemployment was 20 percent in Detroit.

Fifty Years Later, 2008

Democrat Barack Obama is president, and Republican Charlie Crist is governor of Florida. Wars are still going on from Iraq to Afghanistan. Another recession is leveling off, and unemployment nationwide averages 9 percent.

"Time went on, and we wanted to find a home," said Jean.

"In Melrose Park, they were building new homes and within a price range we could afford. We looked at the plans and chose one. They finally got it finished, and we moved in. A million dollars couldn't have made me happier. We bought brand-new furniture, and I was happy as a clam. Melrose Park—same name as the up-north town where we met. In 1959 we moved into that home, and the same year, Mark was born. I stayed home as a mom and took care of him. We didn't go anyplace for eighteen months. I was afraid to get a babysitter. I kept hearing from everyone that you need to have another child, can't have just one. So close to eight years later, Stephanie was born in 1967. I stayed home and took care of the kids. I love the kids, but I always took care of Ed first. This man has always been first, last, and always."

"We lived eighteen years in Melrose Park, then moved to Davie for seventeen years, and then to our present community in Port St. Lucie," Ed said.

They have been through tough health issues and survived. They still are on the go a lot and do most things together, the way they like it.

"So," I ask, *"what's your take on marriage?"*

Jean: Ask yourself this question: "Would you do anything in the world for this person?" If they don't understand, or hesitate, they shouldn't get married. If a couple needs help, then get counseling by a religious person, and do it early on.

Ed: Too many things can pull marriages apart. One thing: both are working. Also computers can interfere with conversation. Lack of communication is one big reason.

Jean: There is not much togetherness among couples today. Sit down and talk with one another every day. There are so many things that I need to talk to Ed about and vice versa. Be aware of the other person's feelings. If they are sensitive, react accordingly. When Ed and I were going together, I was very sensitive, coming from a dysfunctional family. I used to think Ed thought everything was a joke. Actually, when you're oversensitive, you're thinking only of yourself. Now I laugh my head off but at nothing that would hurt the other. Laugh at yourself.

Ed: They say if you can get through the first five years of marriage, then you're on the way. It's like a training field for young couples.

Jean: When children come along, you have to enter that in. Stay home and take care of them.

Ed: Money and politics can draw marriages apart. They can't seem to agree between one another. There are other outside influences, too, which can affect a marriage.

Jean: Parents sometimes can influence one of the kids who may be weak. Take your kids to church, and don't have kids who are turned loose and don't have a lot of direction.

Married people need to work on that together. Our faith made our marriage stronger. I think very little religion or a lack of faith is not good for a marriage. I see people who don't take their vows seriously.

Ed: When we took our vows, we said we're going to do things. We do it. We follow through.

Jean: Marriages fail sometimes because people can be selfish, where it's an "I, me, and my" sort of thing. They think of themselves before anyone else; lots of times it's both of them.

Ed: I think, too, that the educational system is going in the opposite direction of not teaching morality. We were invited to a wedding, and the mother of the bride and the bride said to us, "We're going to try it out for a couple of months and see if it works." Not a good attitude.

Jean: Picking at faults with one another isn't good. Some can't seem to tolerate one another's faults. Everyone has faults; I don't care how good you are. Learn the other person's habits and accept them. Little things like the tooth-paste stuff gets on other people's nerves, and it shouldn't. After a while habits don't make a difference any more.

Author's note: When I interviewed Jean and Ed, I heard from the start why and how a marriage can become and remain strong. They were so good to let me in on their story,

Two people married over fifty years, and she says today, "I love this man so much."
And he, over fifty years later, remembers her wedding gown—"It was beautiful."

Ruth and Ralph Edwards
November 27, 1950

The key is teamwork.

On November 24, 1950, and for a few days after, the middle and eastern part of our country experienced one of the most destructive storms up to that time. The high winds of Hurricane Frieda, large variations in barometer readings, and snow affected Indiana and Pennsylvania and from Lake Erie to Washington DC.

But, on Monday, the twenty-seventh, in Syracuse, New York, at St. Mary's Church on Bellevue Avenue, a marriage was taking place, unaffected by anything going on outside. Ruth and Ralph were married with their immediate family present. Ralph's parents and grandmother were there, having come in from upstate Parishville. His sister, Kathryn, and her husband, Jack, remained in Toledo as they had a baby girl, and Jack was attending the University of Toledo. Ruth's younger sister, Jo Anne, and her husband, Homer, were there, as was her older sister, Frances, who was the maid of honor. The best man was Bill Cowans, a coworker of Ralph's. Hugh Hawkes, Ruth's cousin, took photos. After the ceremony everyone went to Liverpool for dinner. Ruth had made the arrangements, and everything was very nice. Afterward, someone took them to the train station and they headed for Toledo, first stop, Buffalo.

The Statler Hotel at the time was one of the most luxurious places to stay in Buffalo. Ellsworth Milton (E. M.) Statler had started his business there in 1908 and built another hotel in 1923. One of the hotel's claims to fame was having a bath and a radio in every room. The one Ruth and Ralph stayed in was the one with the famed Statler towers, a must-see architectural site. The Statler name was famous for fine lodgings. The promotional brochure *In Buffalo, It's the Statler* said it was located on Delaware Avenue and Niagara Square and the rates were five dollars for a single and seven fifty for a double, with a garage nearby.

"It was the finest hotel in Buffalo," said Ralph, "and unbeknownst to either of us, my mother's uncle, Al Dunn, was head bartender there. He could mix a drink that would match the color of your necktie. The next day we went on to Toledo to meet Kathryn, Jack, and the new baby."

That was sixty-four years ago.

"Ruth and I were born in small towns. Ruth was born in Manchester, New York, and raised there, and graduated from Manchester High School."

Ruth, Frances, and JoAnne O'Harrigan's family was active in community affairs. Their dad, Neal O'Harrigan, worked for the Lehigh Valley Railroad and was village clerk of Manchester–Shortsville, New York, for many years. Their mom was Esther Hawkes, also from Manchester. Neal's sisters—Loretta, Helen, and Margaret—lived a block away. Ruth was close to Aunt Helen, and they visited a lot over their lifetimes. Much of their family was close by in the western New York state small town.

According to census records, Neal lived from 1895 to 1978 and Esther from 1898 to 1970, and Aunt Helen lived until the age of ninety-three. She is buried in the St. Rose Church Cemetery in Shortsville, New York. The *Shortsville Enterprise* was the local newspaper, and in researching Ruth, I found an entry in 1945 about her dad: "Neal O'Harrigan was ill with the grippe." That was the same newspaper that printed: "The fellow who always does everything under the sun, always has shadows under his eyes." Hmmm. Ruth's lineage goes back to that area. A man named Short from Honeoye established the town of Shortsville because he liked the stream and countryside there. He built a flour mill and then a sawmill. The railroads came through eventually and joined with the Manchester area for growth.

"I was born in St. Lawrence County and graduated from Parishville Hopkinton Central," said Ralph. "There were thirteen of us in the class who graduated. Well, shortly after that, I knew I was going to be drafted into the army. My father said, 'You do not want to be in the infantry like I was in France during World War I,' so my mother suggested that I apply for something different."

Ralph's dad, Ralph Sr., had been at the Battle of Saint-Mihiel, France, in 1918, under General Pershing's command, and didn't want to wish that on anyone. It was one of the first times the Germans had used chlorine gas.

"My dad had been wounded as an infantryman there. He and my mother were both pushing me not to be drafted, so I signed up for the air force. My mother wrote letters for me, which were required, and I was accepted and then spent two years as an aviation cadet. I went west and graduated from Carlsbad Army Air Force Base as a bombardier. Right after that I went home on a fifteen-day leave that included travel by train and bus both ways. On the way back through Norman, Oklahoma, we heard horns blowing and sirens going, and saw people blocking the road. The war was over! Lucky me. I could sign up for three more years, or if I didn't, I'd be discharged at the 'convenience of the government.'

"On the way home I stopped in Chicago with some friends I had met in the service, and then with seven dollars in my pocket and a train ticket in hand, I returned home to Parishville. My folks met and greeted me in nearby Potsdam, and I told them about the 'fifty-two/twenty,' which was a government program. A veteran home from the service had fifty-two weeks to get a job and would be given twenty dollars a week while he was looking for a job. Wow! I thought I'd try that…rest and relax."

His mother said, "Fine. I've enrolled you in Clarkson College. You start in three days."

"So much for fifty-two/twenty. I started Clarkson three days after I got home and thought I'd be an electrical engineer. My father had studied through ICS (International Correspondence School) in electrical power. I found out that you had to be super smart in math to be in electrical engineering, and that was not my forte. Took me two years to figure that out, and at that time, I thought I'd quit before they threw me out."

Ralph went a few miles south and continued at Syracuse University night school. He applied for a job at Carrier, got it, found a room on Delaware Avenue in Syracuse, and in addition to night school, worked as a junior engineer at Carrier. The apartment house had four bedrooms and a bath, all rented to young working men. Ralph lived there for several years. He frequently ate his meals in the University cafeteria.

"I noticed several tables occupied by young women who appeared a little more mature than the typical college coed. The 'older gals' were in slacks, seemed more serious, and interested me. Someone told me that they were mostly retired from the service—a lot of nurses—and getting advanced degrees under the GI Bill of Rights. One of them caught my eye as she was a little bit better looking than the others, a little bit better figure than the others, and someone I'd like to meet," said Ralph.

Ruth had graduated from high school in Manchester, was in love, married, and waiting for the war to be over. That happened, but her husband didn't return. He was on the aircraft carrier *Wasp* and was shot down and lost in the battle of the Coral Sea near Guadalcanal. He was killed in September 1942. She was a young widow and decided to go to Syracuse University to become a teacher. She hung out with women closer to her age, and they had meals together. Ruth knew this man had looked at her several times while she was eating in the cafeteria. He looked nice and not dangerous.

"One of the times I had my eye on her," said Ralph, "she was sitting alone, so being a little brazen, I asked her if I could sit beside her with my tray. She said sure, and we chatted away. She was very easy to talk to, and I found her to be very mature—and as I said, she had a good figure. I told her that I'd be eating there often and maybe I'd join her, and she said OK. I did just that, and our talking was interesting. I asked her if she wanted to go to a nearby bar to have a beer, and she said OK. Over a period of time I found out more about her. She was a few years older than I was, and she laughed at my jokes. When she didn't have a date with someone who had a car, we'd eat together and then go nearby to have a beer together.

"I made up my mind rather quickly that I wasn't as mature as I thought I was. I was just barely smart enough to be around her and had to be very careful in showing myself and not coming across as having an inflated ego. Apparently it worked for a while, as we dated quite a bit. Ruth always smiled a lot. She listened well. We used to talk a lot about heredity versus environment. I was an 'environment' person. We'd be at the bar, putting a nickel in the jukebox to dance, and we'd talk about that and about one of her courses, 'Marriage and the Family.' She got an A-plus in it. Ruth thought that heredity was a stronger influence, and for the early years, some of our philosophical views were different. Now, however, I've been reading a lot about the same subjects and I know heredity is the most important.

"I knew I had to get a set of wheels. I had saved some money while I was in the service and had had my parents hang on to it for me. So, I did just that…bought an old car. Ruth and I went for rides on our days off and would stop for ice cream or someplace else for something. She didn't always care for church lawn specials, but we kept going together.

"Ruth often went home to Canandaigua for the weekend with one of her friends, and she either got a ride or took the bus back to Syracuse for the school week. I decided one Sunday I'd drive down to her place and bring her back to Syracuse. I wasn't aware that she often had a boyfriend bring her back. But, that particular weekend when I did go, she was happy to see me rather than take the bus. This went on for a while. One day I figured out one of the best ways to impress her…to show maturity… was to quit my job and go to Syracuse U full time. She was going to have a degree soon, and I was going for one, too."

Ruth did graduate from Syracuse, and Ralph thought that it would be the end of their relationship, as she would probably find a job elsewhere. But, surprise, she got a job at Frozen Foods in Syracuse and therefore was staying in the area. While she was working there, she applied for teaching jobs and was hired by Cherry Road School just outside of Syracuse.

A Little Bit of History

A bit about the jobs that Ruth and Ralph had in the late 1940s. Carrier, where Ralph worked, was a leader in air-conditioning and refrigeration. The company dated back to 1902 when a Cornell graduate engineer, Willis Carrier, designed the first air conditioner when he was only twenty-eight years old. Cherry Road School was actually built on a former cherry orchard that was owned by a family named

Parsons. The great-aunt, Marion Parsons, was principal there for twenty-five years, retiring in. She may have been the principal when Ruth was a teacher. The book *The Brass Bell* tells the story of the school's history; the school still exists today. Ruth received a nice letter from Miss Parsons when Ruth quit teaching there.

"During the years we were together, I became head over heels in love with her," Ralph continued. "Ruth, on the other hand, was and is a very private person and never let on too much where I stood with her. We drove up to meet my parents and then to Paul Smith's to meet my sister, Kathryn, Jack, and their family. I went to meet her family, and she introduced me to her aunts. They were three old maids who lived in Manchester, her father's sisters. They were what you might call 'lace-curtain Irish ladies.' If I ever met any, they were them...three lovely ladies.

"Ruth was number one with them, so they all accepted me. A couple of years later, I went to see my parents alone, and I was talking to my mother. Dad was out at a lodge meeting. She asked me how Ruth and I were doing, and I told her that I loved Ruth and that she was the only girl I had ever really fallen in love with. My mother said, 'Then you had better marry her.' The same kind of thing happened a few weeks later in North Syracuse when my sister and her husband returned for a birthday celebration. They asked me to attend, and I did. We chatted and Jack told me, 'Kaye and I have been talking, and we're wondering about you and Ruth...if you're going to get married or not.' Well, I told them that I thought we'd get married before Christmas. I hadn't even asked Ruth yet and, during the three years we went together, never even mentioned marriage."

In late summer, Ralph and Ruth were picnicking in Bellevue Park and were walking back to the car.

"I think we should probably get married about Thanksgiving time," Ralph said to Ruth.

"Ruth responded by looking at me and saying nothing. We both returned to our own apartments and I didn't know if I was getting married or not, or if I was pushing it too quickly."

A week later Ruth announced, "I've made arrangements for you to meet Father Carry at the church so you can have lessons and have made arrangements for a date to get married in the church. I think we should get an engagement ring, and we should go to my aunt's in Rochester and go to a really nice jewelry store I know of."

Wedding plans were made. Ruth and Ralph did go to a nice jewelry store in Rochester and picked out a diamond ring. She put the ring on right there in the store, and they were engaged. Then Ruth made the other arrangements for the wedding meal in Liverpool, too.

That was all in the 1950s—the marriage and the beginning years of raising a family.

1950

1950 was the year the Korean conflict started with General Douglas MacArthur as commander in chief. President Harry Truman announced the approval of the hydrogen bomb, and genius Albert Einstein announced he was against the whole thing. Hopalong Cassidy, at fifty-five years old, led the Macy's Day Parade. During this era Mother Teresa came into the public eye, and the first credit card was issued (Diner's Club). Bob Hope made his first appearance on TV, Peter Pan opened on Broadway, Paul Harvey broadcasted and Peanuts was created as a soon to be favored cartoon. Jackie Robinson signed the biggest contract with the Dodgers for $35,000 a year, and Sugar Ray Robinson was middleweight champion. These were the baseball days of Connie Mack, Joe DiMaggio, and Whitey Ford. The fifties were a decade of morals and manners.

Ruth was teaching, making money, and Ralph was going to school but didn't really like it, and the GI bill was going to run out. So his idea was to quit Syracuse University and get back to work full time at Carrier Corporation in the plant layout department. "Made me feel pretty good that I was going to contribute financially," he said.

They lived in Ruth's apartment for about a year, saving money and looking for a small house. They found one in Fayetteville, near Syracuse, for $11,800 and a GI loan for 4 percent.

"We moved into a brand-new home on Hunt Drive. The second year we lived there, Ruth was pregnant with Debbie. I was all of a sudden mature with the load we were carrying. I was sure she was going to be a boy, but when I looked at our baby girl, I bought in. We lived at 321 Hunt Drive for five years. I finished off the upstairs for our oldest daughter, Debbie. Then Kathy was born. My grandmother was visiting and sleeping with Kathy upstairs. Debbie, two years older, decided she would have no part of her new bedroom and said how hot it was; hence I installed a large window conditioner. We then started looking for a little larger house and found a ranch on Dawley Road on a wider and deeper lot with a lovely farm behind it. The house required a bit of work. The things I learned in the first house I put to use in the second house. I learned about cellar pipe leaks, peeling paint, broken-up driveways, and things like that."

Ruth, Debbie, and Kathy enjoyed the neighborhood and were happy with the schools. Eventually, after about ten years of working for Carrier, Ralph decided he wasn't getting ahead fast enough and had met several guys who were doing pretty well; they had a nice road ahead of them. "So," said Ralph, " I started looking for another job. I went to Rochester, New York, and applied to several: Bausch and Lomb, Consolidated, and Delco, part of General Motors. I took the job at Delco when the girls were in elementary school."

Ruth stayed in Fayetteville until the school year finished, and Ralph went ahead and established a new home base in Rochester. Delco was a fine place to work, and both Ruth and Ralph made a lot of good friends in the neighborhood and through work. Ruth was in a TWIG group which raised money and volunteered at Rochester General. They enjoyed the volunteerism as well as the social aspects. Playing bridge was a favorite pastime, and soon she became an in-home tutor for many years for a young lad with autism, one of the first students to be identified with the condition.

"My father had two mentors in his work career who made a tremendous difference. They took him under their wing, advised him as to which course to take, what kind of direction to take, and it all paid off," Ralph said. "Well, the same thing happened to me at General Motors. My first mentor was Dave Salomon. He was wiser, more intelligent, and his mentoring helped a great deal. GM was very different from Carrier as many workers had advanced degrees and were people who had made it in the business world. It all helped me. I liked my job at Delco much better, and I learned that if you're happy when you come home from work, then Momma is happier. And when Momma is happier, then everyone is happier. That made a difference. I liked my job, and I also took a liking for Carl Foucht, a farm boy from Ohio and an electrical engineer who went to Harvard for advanced work. He was very low key and seemed to solve a math or logic problem by just squinting his eyes at it These mentors made a great deal of difference for me."

During these years, there was playtime, too. Ralph was a hunter, as was his father and some of his pals at work. Years before, in 1915, the Emporium Forestry Company from Emporium, Pennsylvania, bought about three hundred thousand acres in St. Lawrence County, New York, and built a town: Conifer. A sawmill and the New York Central railroad came along to produce, load up, and distribute lumber all over the country. Part of this huge area, about two thousand acres, was leased out, and the Sampson Pond Club was formed with about thirty hunters who thoroughly enjoyed each other and the food they lugged in or made there. They stayed overnight for days at a time, hunting in November of each year. Ruth always noted that the hunting week ended a few days prior to their wedding anniversary, and that meant a few days away for the two of them.

"Well," said Ralph, "GM started to get hit by the Japanese motor car industry. GM had had over fifty percent of that industry but was starting to feel the pinch. The pressure was put on then, telling engineers that when we were sixty,

we needed to retire. They did put out some nice motiva-
tion: the kicker. GM gave us the Social Security equivalent
for the years of sixty to sixty-two. I was a little concerned
about retirement, but it was and is wonderful. I had a
lot of hobbies and interests from downhill skiing to sailing to working on the car to some woodworking. Ruth's
aunts had a cottage on Canandaigua Lake, and we could
go there anytime. My folks had a place at Star Lake in the
Adirondack Mountains and we went there, too. I thought
about getting a job, but we had money coming in and we
were OK. We bought a place in Boynton Beach right on
the Intracoastal Waterway in Florida, and it was about a
twenty-minute walk to the ocean. It was lovely; we kept it for
sixteen years. We had down-sized from our split-level house
in suburban Rochester to a condo, which was lovely, too.
We got there because one day my daughter Kathy caught
me when I was on a ladder with an extension cord and a
saw, and she said, 'No more.' And that's how we went to the
condo on Running Brook. Life was good, full of hobbies,
friends, pastimes, wintering in the South, and watching
our three lovely granddaughters grow."

Then Ruth was diagnosed with spinal stenosis, so they
started looking for a place that would be better suited to
them.

"We'd better start looking for places for old people,"
said Ralph. They checked out places and kinds of homes
and settled on an apartment in a lovely, upscale multiser-
vice community in Pittsford, another Rochester suburb. not
too far from Kathy and John. "We moved into a beautiful
apartment, eight years ago now, and it was a smart move.
Didn't know it at the time, but it was."

Ruth and Ralph will celebrate their sixty-fourth wedding anniversary in November, and Ralph still tells their children that when he and Ruth were going together and they'd look down that long tunnel for the future, they both saw the same light.

"We talked about the future a lot. We had a lot of the same goals. One was to do well in our jobs. Ruth helped me a lot with my clothing selections, picked out furniture, and in general decorated our homes. Ruth had more money than I, early on. She even shopped at Flah's. We assumed that she would be a stay-at-home mom; we wanted to have children. Ruth was thirty-one when she became pregnant and then did stay home and raise our girls. I never knew anyone who wanted to be a mom as much as Ruth did.

"When we lived in Fayetteville and we had Debbie, I said to Ruthie, 'We have to be careful with our money.' Well, starting then she became knowledgeable of the price of ketchup at three different stores, shopped the stores, saved coupons and became very good with money. We both started to listen and talk, read money magazines, and talk with Carl about some of his investments. We got into some good ones, too, and some bad ones. It was a wonderful time to invest back then," continued Ralph.

"I think our marriage worked for a lot of reasons. We're both from small towns, and both of our parents were big frogs in small ponds and were very respected. I was close to my sister and parents, and we were a closely knit family. My sister said it first and best when she stated that she and I had been blessed with the parents we had. I had also said that most of my adult life I have attempted to be half the man my father was—still trying. Ruth was very close to her father, mother, and sisters, and they, too, were a closely knit family. I think that has a lot to do with it. In my opinion I have always thought that Ruth and I were pretty even as far as 'being the boss' in the family. We do talk about people who maybe don't have a good marriage. We think the key is teamwork, and as I said, when we look down that tunnel, we see the same light."

It's hard to believe that Ruth and Ralph are senior seniors! Married the longest of the interviewed people, they still look at each other the way I imagine they did 64 years ago. He's a real conversationalist and is interested in just about everything that moves…railroads, planes, boats, cars, deer…and whatever subject you want to bring up. Ruth listens and smiles at her husband.

Ruth Edwards passed away in November, 2014.

Sue and Joe Bruschetti
August 4, 1962

The extended family kept the family close and accountable.

The towns in Long Island are almost all connected and almost share the same histories—they were settled by people coming from the city encouraged by the Long Island Railroad, which helped the towns grow. Many towns were named after Indian groups who had lived there or by sea captains active in the waters surrounding the island. Other towns were named after waterfowl, fish, wild horses, the Dutch, the English and postwar Jews. Two Nassau County towns in this story are Massapequa meaning "Great Water Land", or wetlands, to early North American Indians and Seaford, named after Captain Sea*man*. When people in suburban towns of fifteen thousand to thirty thousand people spread out, they formed new towns near-by, just adding a "West" or a "North" to the town's name. In the twentieth century, first-wave immigrants arriving at Ellis Island found their way to a home with a piece of land, a safer place to raise their families. The Italians, Irish, Germans, and Slavs came with their extended families and, for the most part, stayed in the area. Consequently generations of families lived near each other and stayed tight. There was a big Italian influence on Long Island, Sue and Joe said.

Joe's father was born in Messina, Italy, and his mom in Basel, Switzerland. When they came to this country in the early 1920s, they were going to speak "Americanny." They met at night school, preparing to get their citizenship. His mom was a governess for wealthy people involved with Grace Shipping. She had an unhappy childhood and was delighted to come here. His dad came here for a better life as a carpenter. He had been in the Italian army during World War I.

This family sketch was fairly common among people on Long Island or anywhere near the point of arrival from Europe. They were hopeful people who worked very hard and passed on those ethics.

Sue's dad always worked two jobs, and her mom stayed at home, passing on good virtues to her six children. When Sue's brother was killed in Vietnam in 1968, they did what they always did: hung together and took care of each other. That family influence kept Sue's brother as part of the family forever. It was the way it was, in larger, close-knit Catholic families.

Long Island towns had everything needed to keep people there: beaches to the north and the south; cultural and sporting events an hour away by rail; and schools, churches, and small industry. Aunts, cousins, and grandparents lived nearby and knew everything about each other. People typically stayed in their homes for a long time, building an addition, knocking out walls, finishing an upstairs or a basement, putting in a backyard pool—all with home-grown help. Some families took in a boarder to help defray costs, ensuring that they would be able to stay in their home and close to family who might be down the street or in the next town. Families were families no matter how extended they were.

Sue's girlfriend Linda always talked about her brother's buddy, Joe—when he was coming over, how cute he was. "This went on for a while," said Sue, "and eventually the arrangement was made that I was to be at my girlfriend's home, accidentally. I went over and met him. It was awkward for me, and I didn't think Joe even noticed. We were talking, and I did think he was cute. Then it started to pour rain. I had walked over to Linda's house, so Joe said to me, 'Do you want me to give you a ride home?' I thought about going with a stranger a bit but did take the ride home. It was near New Year's, and I think Joe asked if I wanted to go out."

"I asked you to go to a movie," said Joe, "and I said I'd call you as soon as I can. I had no idea I was being set up. I had called my friend Kenny and said I would swing by. No idea that I was being observed. I thought Sue was cute... pretty, actually. And I did offer her the ride home, called her, and we went to a movie."

Sue said, "When I got home from Linda's, I flew into the house and said, 'Mom, I met someone. He's so cute; he's so cute.' She asked what his name was, and I said it was

Joe Bruschetti. Her questions were 'What kind of a name is that?' and 'How old is he?' All I was thinking about was how cute he was, and here she was thinking name and age.

"We both had dates with others for New Year's Eve, but we did the movie and talked a lot on the phone. I'm the oldest of six, so our house was crawling with activities. My mom thought he was too old for me, so we never really told them Joe's real age and cut off a couple of years. I was eighteen, and Joe had been in the navy for four years…maybe a little worldly for me. But I thought he was wonderful, and Mom would say, 'Who is he, Saint Joseph?' I would tell my mother not to worry about anything. We started to date exclusively, and my parents set pretty strict curfews, which we abided by."

Joe said, "I made sure she was home on time. We'd sit at the kitchen table and talk; I really became very involved with her family."

"I was finishing high school when I met Joe, and a few months later we became engaged."

"I worked in electronics in the navy, and carried on with that as an electronics tester for Republic Aviation. Republic went on strike, and within two weeks, I was hired by Pan American."

"So when we planned our wedding, the date was based on when Joe could have time off. That was the way if you were new at work, and he was new at Pan Am.

"I said I was the eldest in a large family. Well, when we had my engagement party, my mother was pregnant with my youngest brother, and we had to have a babysitter for the wedding. That little brother actually got away with murder. He's well over six foot now, but is still, always, the baby.

"Our wedding was at a ten o'clock Mass on Saturday morning, August 4, 1962, at Maria Regina Catholic Church, on Jerusalem Avenue, in Seaford," said Sue. "My dad always worked two jobs and worked hard for money so that all in the family could be outfitted for the wedding. I went to a photography studio someone told me about that sold gowns at half price if you had them do the pictures. That was nice. At the time, I worked at Liberty Mutual in Lynbrook—my first job. I brought home fifty dollars a week and carpooled with four others, which most people did then. Everyone at the time was getting married, and conversations in the office were about marriages. All the girls had daily calendars and marked off so many days to the wedding...some had three hundred days to wait, others seven days. It wasn't difficult to borrow anything from anyone. I borrowed a veil with a double-decker crown."

Joe said, "When we went to the fiftieth anniversary party at the clubhouse here in Savanna Club, most celebrants had pictures of their weddings, and it was interesting to see them."

"We all looked so much alike—hairdos on both the girls and the guys, different colors for the bridesmaids, and no strapless gowns," said Sue. Maria Regina Catholic Church was founded in 1955 and has a large parish today. It was then, and is still, a lovely church.

"I got there early, and I was pacing back and forth," said Joe. "I was nervous. The altar boy's bike was there, so I took it, rode it around, and worked off some steam, all in my white jacket. Well, in church I remember her coming down the aisle, and she was beautiful. We got to the altar and I was shaking so badly, especially one leg."

Sue said, "I thought, what the heck? His leg was jumping. The Mass went on and on. The priest who was supposed to marry us didn't; another did. We were so disappointed when another priest did."

"We got through it," said Joe.

"We went to a reception at a little restaurant. It was seven-fifty a person for a full-course dinner, which we had saved for. We just didn't have much money," said Sue.

"I don't think either one of us finished our dinner," Joe added. "We went around talking, and besides that, the photographer kind of pushed us into a system of taking pictures."

"He was terrible," said Sue, "and we were busy talking to people. Joe has a very small family. He has one sister and her husband and two little kids and a few cousins. I was the first one in our family to get married, so he was meeting a lot of my family for the first time."

"As I said, neither one of us did eat," said Joe. "After the reception, we went to her house to change, and on the way to the hotel, we stopped at a diner to eat. The waitress saw us dressed up and asked what was the occasion. I told her we just got married. She said, 'This is your wedding dinner?'"

"We honeymooned at Mount Airy in the Pocono Mountains, Pennsylvania, and returned to an apartment in Massapequa. We signed a year's lease for one hundred ten dollars a month, which was at that time equal to Joe's weekly salary, as he had taken a pay cut to go to Pan Am. As soon as we got our apartment, Joe started doing shift work, the midnight shift. The shifts changed on a monthly basis, but then, right away, I was alone at night. The place was so quiet. I had been used to a large family and a full house. Massapequa was one town over from my parents' home. I was scared. My defense was I had a can of hairspray under my pillow. I was going to get that guy—anyone who intruded—with that."

Joe added, "It was an upstairs apartment in a private home, so I was OK with that."

"The landlady had made it perfectly clear: no children in the apartment. I was still working, but after six months of marriage, I found that I was pregnant. In my job you couldn't work past six months pregnant either, so we actively started looking for a house. Well, there were so many delays with the house thing. We had the baby, Joe was still doing shift work, and I often went to my mother's. At times my sister or brother would babysit.

"We found a home in Babylon, a little farther away, and lived there twenty-six years. We had Diane in 1963, John in 1965, and Jeannie in 1969. They all went to public schools, the elementary school was right down the block. I was a stay-at-home mom until Jeanne was in fourth grade."

"Our house was a Cape Cod," said Joe, "with an unfinished upstairs dormer. When John was born, I finished the dormer bedrooms with a bath upstairs, and it was nice. I knocked out a wall, raised the floors, and worked around the house. Everything was for the kids and the family."

"When Joe was working shifts at Pan Am, it'd be when the kids came home from school. 'Be quiet, your father's sleeping' and 'Where's Daddy? Is he at work or sleeping?'" said Sue. "I went to part-time work at schools and a department store, and did some volunteering. The whole thing about women working back then was that the family was not to be disturbed. Be home when the kids came home. I picked up my paycheck at one window at the store where I worked, and then went to another and paid the bill. Since I worked in the girls' department, we were always very well dressed.

"After the kids were old enough, things were more flexible, and I was able to work a full-time job. My first job was in an office furniture store as purchasing agent. I was approached and asked if I would be interested in a job as office manager for an insurance brokerage firm in Manhattan. I nervously accepted, and there I was in my own office on the fourteenth floor of the Lincoln Building, directly across from Grand Central Station, and with a view of the Empire State Building. Commuting was fun at first and then very tiring. The firm relocated its offices to Garden City, Long Island, which was only forty-five minutes from home by car. I stayed there for a few years until Joe was hired by Delta and we moved to Georgia."

"It was a simpler life back then," said Joe. "You could buy easier, and money went further. Eventually we had two cars."

"The entertainment was family. Everything was done at our house," Sue said, "and we made everything for all occasions. If it was a shower or whatever, we'd be doing potato salad or meatballs for whatever."

Joe said, "We didn't do a lot when we first were married. We'd get a six-pack of beer, go to a friend's house for cards and an Entenmann's cake, bring the playpen. That was it. We had a lot of friends."

"I didn't come from much, but I had everything I thought I needed," said Sue. "Our wants were simple. When my parents moved from the Bronx to Long Island, they didn't even have a driver's license and, after that, had the one car."

"But," added Joe, "at one point each of our kids had cars. There were five cars in our driveway when they were all living at home."

"Life was good. Diane was married to an air force man and moved to Texas. John finished University of Buffalo, had an apartment, and was on his own. Only Jeannie lived with us," Sue said.

A Little Bit of History

Airlines have been a tremendously important industry in our country, in our world. They all started small with one goal, usually as a vision of one person. Pan Am founder Juan Trippe wanted to make it possible for the average American to fly. He also wanted to fly between countries, particularly those to the south of us. The very first flight was a mail delivery from Key West to Puerto Rico. Delta started as the Huff Daland Dusters of Georgia, the first of its kind in the agricultural business of crop dusting. Evolving into Delta, it started carrying passengers and the first flight was for five passengers at a speed of ninety miles an hour. In the early 1940's, before Joe's work entry, it moved its head-quarters to Atlanta, Georgia, and began acquiring other companies. Because of the company's cargo—people—the technology used for every piece and phase of flying had to be in A-plus condition and 100 percent accurate. Joe's jobs related to that.

"Pan Am was going out of business," said Joe, "and I had made it through a few layoffs. I had been a mechanic for seven years and a supervisor for twenty-two years. The economy on Long Island at the time was not good. United was laying off, too. I went to Delta Air for an interview and was hired as an instructor. Delta had picked up all Pan Am Airbus A31's planes, and the best thing for them was to take the people who knew their planes. The job was in Atlanta, so I left and got an apartment in Atlanta with another guy. Sue stayed in Long Island for about six months to sell the house."

Sue recalled, "Joe flew back and forth for the weekend from Atlanta to NYC. He just did it; now it seems insane. I was planning the move and including Jeannie in our move. But she said she was going to stay in New York. She became engaged and did stay. That was devastating to me, horrible—having to leave her there and move on. But move we did and went back and forth, visiting. For Jeannie's wedding, we were in Georgia, no house on Long Island where the wedding was to be. A girlfriend said we could use her house for the pictures. The day of the wedding there was a northeaster, and she was on the water. Interesting. A storm, but the sun was shining by the end of the day. The two things that were godsends were first, the people who bought our house on Long Island were going to make an apartment upstairs that would have a separate entrance, and it would be a rental. So Jeannie ended up renting the apartment for a couple of years in her own former home. The other godsend was that we were able to go back and forth on free flights.

"We lived in an apartment for about a year in Atlanta. Then we saw a model house that we liked. The builder changed some of it for us, and we had a beautiful home.

Times were different, and we got so much for our money.
It was an all-brick ranch, three thousand square feet on
a three-quarter acre. There was a building boom in the
area, and the builders wanted to sell houses. Pan Am had
a lot of workers who had come south and now worked for
Delta, whom we knew. We had a nice group of friends in
Fayetteville, Georgia, just south of the airport. We lived
there for nine years. We always had dogs and brought the
last one from Georgia to Florida when we moved south
once again."

Joe picks up the story. "Sue's parents had lived in South
Florida since the nineteen eighties, and we would visit
them with our kids. It was our vacation. First in Stuart,
then Port Salerno, and then, when they were looking
around the Treasure Coast, Sue's mom fell in love with
this community. They were looking at it with another couple, and Sue's mom's friend loved it too. Her dad wanted
to know what was wrong with the place they were living
in at the time. The friend wrote a check for them, and for
my in-laws, of a thousand dollars each as a down payment,
and they ended up living next door to each other. They
had known each other since childhood in the Bronx; the
Williams's still live here. In the year two thousand, we
bought here, too."

*So what's your take on staying together for over fifty years? And why
do you think some couples cannot?*
Sue: From the very beginning, it was one hundred ten
percent family
Joe: I was absorbed into the family. I'm like a big brother
to her sisters and brothers.

Sue: We're close to family and have a lot of younger siblings. There's a constant buffer of people nearby, and that
helps marriages stay together—always supporting each other and trying to find the humor in sometimes not-so-funny
situations.

Joe: There is a big family influence on us. Even when we
moved, we still had close family ties. Someone would just
drop in with Dunkin' Donuts and visit.

Sue: When my mother was growing up, her three sisters
were close by, so I had close cousins as well. You always
had someone to talk to about those petty little things that
would make me want to say or think, 'Something got under
my skin.' But I always had my mother to share with.

Joe: You can have petty differences…pride…but you still
love each other. You can have a difference of opinions. But
nowadays it seems they stand their ground and leave—a
throw-away marriage.

Sue: It's good to have someone else to account to. Today,
some marriages break because they think it doesn't affect
other people; they're moving on separately.

Joe: Everything is temporary today. People bail out; they
have no patience. It's 'me, me, me' that make marriages
fail. Marriage is a commitment. Take the good with the
bad. You are not always going to agree. Put your pride aside.

Sue: I think religion has a lot to do with it. I'm not saying only Catholic but a spiritual life. Pray about it, go to
church; take your kids to church.

Joe: Family influence carried on to kids. We hear a lot
of horror stories about how marriages don't work out. Our
three kids all stayed married and take their kids to church,
practice their Christian values. They work hard at all of

this. They're caring, loving people, feeding the homeless and doing other helpful things. Everything used to be a lot simpler; everyone around you was in the same boat, and there didn't seem to be a lot of demands.

Sue: We are Catholic and just don't get divorced. Marriage is a sacrament and commitment. It would have disappointed Nana and my parents if we did. A woman working is the norm today. They have invested a lot of time and money in their careers. Spending so much time out of the home and seeing coworkers more than their husband or children can cause problems at home; there are so many temptations. Life today is much harder for women than it was in the fifties or sixties. They are expected to do it all now.

But now there are divorces. People move away from extended family and, chalk it up to "Oh well, that's the times."

Joe: Society's influences are not the same as they used to be. Marriage is a sacred thing needing patience, love, compromise, and always a good sense of humor.

From the very beginning, it was 110 percent family. No matter what, you knew you were going to stay married. If it was a mother, or my grandmother nana or another family person, there was always someone to answer to.

Bea and Dick Schantz
August 27, 1960

We just knew we were to stay together.

Bea was a freshman at Rochester Institute of Technology, having graduated from Brighton High School in 1957, and Dick was an upperclassman, having graduated from West High in 1954. They met at the snack bar while he was playing bridge.

"He said something casual, like did I want to go out Friday night," said Bea. "Later he told me he kind of liked my legs. Well, the first date we went to the Genesee Park Inn and had a few beers. He said he was broke…had only five dollars, and that's what I had…five dollars. We had two beers and danced. Dick went home with three dollars, and I was broke. Zero.

"We did not have a lot of money to go out. He was paying for his own college education."

They were immersed in Rochester Institute of Technology, a very fine school for a variety of degree programs. Dick and

Bea were there two and a half years together, dating, and in January 1960, they became engaged.

"When that happened, all hell broke loose. Dick and his family were Catholic, and my family and I were Presbyterian. Dick's mother had a stroke…and no one was going to come to our wedding, which we were planning for the summer."

Dick graduated with an organic chemistry degree, and Bea decided to leave school so Dick could continue on to get a master's degree.

"Our wedding was planned for Mt. Hor Presbyterian Church," said Bea, "and when the guys at Dick's fraternity received the invitation, being the young undergraduates that they were, ribbed Dick about the church name.

"The wedding was nice. My cousin was maid of honor, and two girlfriends close to me at the time were brides-maids. I wore a long dress. Dick's best man was Norm, and when we celebrated our fiftieth wedding anniversary, Norm took us around Saratoga. That was just a few years ago and was very nice. Two ushers were fraternity brothers. Dick's brother was Catholic and going to be a priest and couldn't, therefore, be in the wedding.

"His parents, two sisters, and brother did come to the wedding, and the rest of the family joined us at the reception, which was at the Dowd Post. The whole buffet dinner was one hundred fifty dollars, one dollar a person. The nice part about that was we left right the next day for Kentucky, had a short honeymoon, and Dick started graduate school at the University of Kentucky in Lexington. There was nothing good about the next two years. We had no money and couldn't do much. I had never really left home and lived on my own, so I had never cooked and never cleaned. It was just hell for two years. We ended up coming home with a master's degree and a baby. Richard…Rick had been born in 1962."

Bea and Dick returned to Rochester, and Dick started work at Kodak, where he worked the rest of his life. In those days, that's what guys did: they worked at the first place they were hired, usually had great benefits, and became loyal, immersed in the company, usually staying until retirement.

A Little Bit of History

In Dick's time, Eastman Kodak was the largest employer of people in Rochester, New York, and the surrounding area. Rochester ("Flour City"…"Flower City"…"Kodak City"), a city of 330,000 people, was also the home of Xerox, a world leader in xerography. But Kodak was tops in the camera world and had super benefits for "Kodakers," including family movies, baseball, and other sporting events to be involved in. To be employed at Kodak in the mid-twentieth century was to be set for life, so it seemed. In the sixties in Rochester, as in most cities, downtown was an attractive shopping and financial hub. But, in 1964, race riots in the United States occurred. and they lasted for a few days in Rochester's inner city. This exacerbated the flight to the suburbs. Racial issues became topics for everyone. Suburban churches became involved in debates and establishing ways to help minority groups. Bethany Presbyterian Church, which Bea and Dick attended, in suburban Greece was no different.

"Robin was born in 1963, and five years later, Kevin was born. Things were working out just fine. We moved to Greece, and the kids went to Lakeshore School just down the street. Well, we had been married for fourteen or fifteen years, and I wanted to get out and work. Times were changing. It was a new time when women were told that we could do anything we wanted to."

Dick sat her down one day and said, "Look, I make enough money, and you're going to stay home and take care of the children."

"So I did," Bea said, "and I was OK with that. He also said that I could go out to work as long as I was home when the kids got home from school, and he wasn't going to help with the chores. I realized this was right, and we got along fine. We each had our duties and responsibilities."

This principle of marriage was fairly common in those days. Why would a woman work outside the home? The concept of two parents working seemed unnecessary unless there were too many mouths to feed and not enough income, or the family overextended in the home they bought, the cars they drove, or the pricey activities they chose. This didn't seem to happen too often to people born and raised in the 1920s, '30s, and '40s. Couples seemed satisfied with the women working in the home, raising the children the majority of the time, and the man bringing home the bacon and not mopping the floors or putting the children to bed by himself. The concept of going beyond the husband's salary would have been interpreted as just trying to "get ahead of the Joneses." The fulfillment of a woman through a career outside of the home was not a consideration. But that idea was beginning to surface and to be embraced publically.

There were so many activities associated with their church, which were time-consuming and rewarding, too.

They were active in many groups, including RIT alumni; Shipmates, a couples group; Greece Enrichment Group of twenty women, and card clubs. Dick was also usually an officer of the church in some capacity.

"We were very active in church work; he had his things to do, and I had my things to do. Dick was a people person, and that's probably why we were always out with others. Everything always worked out. He had respect for me, and I had respect for him. He never complained about my cooking, unless I made noodles and tuna fish. When he knew that's what was coming, he might say, 'You want to go for dinner?'"

When Kevin was seven or eight years old, there was evidence of learning problems. He was diagnosed with dyslexia. Dick couldn't accept it, found it hard. "Once we had the diagnosis, we put him in the Norman Howard School, and Dick was gradually accepting it," said Bea. "When he took Kevin to school, Dick found out his boss's son was also at Norman Howard School, which made it kind of easier, OK. That was one hurdle that we overcame.

"Dick was very demanding, when the kids were small, that we'd have breakfast and evening dinner together. I really think that was an important aspect in keeping our family together. The kids remember it very well. They also remember our family vacations, which we started in 1990. Every other year we'd go on vacation…all of us. Some were big trips, and as the family grew, everyone went. One year we all went on a cruise; that was when Rick's wife told us she was pregnant. Our first grandchild was coming. Another time we all went to the Outer Banks. It was all fun.

"When we were married twenty-five years, it was kind of tough. That year, 1985, his mother died from a stroke, and my mother also died of a stroke. A rough year. We had two parents to take care of: both of our fathers. Dick's dad was very upset over his wife's death and, in turn, made it difficult for us. Six years later, Dick retired from Kodak, and I was working part time at the Red Cross. A while back, I had worked part time at the drapery shop on Lake Avenue and became experienced with window treatment. 'So Dick,' I said one morning right after he retired, 'I have been making this bed for thirty-five years, so now the last person out makes the bed.' I made rules, too."

Dick was active in RIT alumni activities and was elected president in the mid-1970s. He was chairman of homecoming, president of his fraternity's board of trustees, and alumni designee to the RIT board of trustees. Rochester Institute of Technology was a centerpiece for the couple as they attended many functions there, and after Kevin was well into elementary school, Bea returned to finish her business degree, leaving the house as soon as Kevin boarded the bus, and returning before all three children were home. "It was nice because I went free as Dick was on the Board of Trustees."

A Little Bit of History

If there ever was a school that started as grassroots venture, it was RIT. Its history is fascinating. In 1829, people such as Nathaniel Rochester started Athenaeum to promote literature, science, and the arts. Twenty years later, the Mechanical Literary Association merged with the

Athenaeum, creating an extensive library on a variety of subjects. Then the group joined together intellectually, engaging well-known speakers. In the latter nineteenth century, the school was founded on the concept of providing technical training for skilled workers in industry. The first class was a mechanical drawing class; cost for the first year was eight dollars. Rochester Athenaeum and Mechanics merged in 1901 as a cultural and practical educational institution. It grew quickly and practically, adding a cooperative educational aspect, industrially oriented programs, then photography and printing, day and evening classes, the great National Technical Institute for the Deaf...NTID... programs, distance-learning robotics, sustainability, PhD degrees, and cutting-edge courses, and made a move from the city to suburban Henrietta. Dick and Bea were active in homecoming committees way back in 1966 and then on for many years. When Dick was president of the alumni association, it was only three or so years until the big RIT 150th anniversary. Bob Hope was a speaker.

A good place to stay involved with was Bethany Presbyterian Church, which was established near the corner of Dewey and Stone in Greece, about 1910. It has always been active in outreach programs for those in need, especially those in need in our community. A few decades ago, the Presbyterian women took sewing machines to the migrant camps on a weekly basis so the women could sew clothing. There were women's circles, men's programs, scouting support, fellowship, and curriculum-based children's programs, as well as Two Doors, a community-based after-school program, and the group that Bea now organizes, the Greece Food Shelf.

Over the years I don't believe there has been a department or need area to which Dick and/or Bea haven't devoted their time and service. Their all-time devotion has been to Shipmates, a group of about eighty men and women who stay together for Christian fellowship. Bea and Dick each have served as elder or deacon of the governing bodies of the church. The church and RIT have been centerpieces of their time and energy.

"Dick was interviewed by the *Democrat & Chronicle*, the Rochester newspaper, for an article titled 'Wives of Executives.' They basically were inquiring how wives put up with husbands who are gone a lot," said Bea. "I said, 'He's just Dick to me.' And for some reason the guys at work gave him the raspberry about that remark. 'He's just Dick…he's just Dick to me,' they teased."

Dick and Bea have been members of Shipmates for fifty-one of its fifty-eight-year existence. "The Greece Enrichment Group was my lifesaver as I got out once a month. It was wonderful. That and all of the groups we volunteered in all took time and planning. Dick and I were family oriented and did a lot family wise, too."

After retiring, Dick took up downhill skiing and golf. "He'd be gone for a few days out west or up north skiing. I would go gambling, but he didn't really approve of it. 'You're leaving me home alone again,' Dick said sometimes. But we also had our own little routines. We gave each other space. Dick took up fishing and then got a chartering business on Lake Ontario. He got his captain's license, and the group that hired him would be called a six-pack because you can have six people on our boat. He did that for a while. Sometimes I made meals for people. For a while I also baked pies and brought them to the clients when they went fishing. I didn't go out on the charter. In February of 1996, the boat burned. That winter he kept his boat at a marina, and he had it for sale because it had become too much work. So it burned. He stuck with downhill skiing and golf. I didn't do either. I went to the Y almost every day.

"The best thing we did," she said, "was letting the other do what they wanted to. We gave each other space all the time. I think that is key. There are some couples who do everything together, and I wonder how they'll do later, when they're alone."

The largest tragedy in Bea and Dick's life by far was the sudden death of their youngest child, Kevin. He was in his thirties, driving his motorcycle home from the evening shift at work, and was hit by an elderly man who didn't look where he was going.

One early morning in June, I received a phone call from Bea, my girlfriend and former neighbor. Her voice was quiet but unsteady. "Kevin died this morning. He was in a dreadful accident." There were very few words. I knew exactly how she was feeling, and she knew that I knew, because I, too, had had a son who died far too early. They had been about the same age at death. There is not one day that goes by when a parent's thoughts are not with the child she or he shouldn't have had to bury. But, thank God for God, for he takes care of them.

"You know, both Dick and I were born in Rochester, and our mothers were at Rochester General Hospital at the same time giving birth, but not to us. Dick's mom gave birth to one of his siblings, and my mom had my brother. Rochester General used to be on West Main. Of course that's something we found out much later. He and I have been family oriented all of our lives. We both were always into games with others, doing for others, and being with others. Dick would do anything; he would try anything. He was such a good sport. He loved working outside and had a great vegetable garden when we lived on Lake Meadow all the years we were raising the kids."

Dick died rather suddenly of a brain tumor in the spring of 2011.

"As a widow, it's a whole different ball game. I was supposed to go first, and I thought I would. I didn't want to take care of the books, but I do it now. I had to learn. I am capable of doing it for now. I did adjust. I never thought I could live alone. But I am. I don't think I'd want to go through what I have gone through again. My Bethany family wrapped around me. The Shipmates were there for us when Dick died and before that when our son died. It's a 'deep in the faith' thing. I couldn't have lived without them. I think Dick would agree with that. I believe that is another thing that kept us together: faithful church groups. Sometimes I get upset with some of them because of some reason or other...just like a family. If my own children did something wrong, I wouldn't just up and leave them."

Bea took hold of what she had to do soon after her husband's death.

"I don't get down on myself. There are some people who do. They say, 'I don't know what to do.' I am busy all the time.

"I think Dick would say the same thing about why our marriage was as long lasting as it was. The best thing we did was let the other do what they wanted to. And we both like people. Dick, as I said, loved to talk to anyone and everyone. He used to walk around our neighborhood and kind of just check up on everyone that he saw…in a healthy, caring way. Me, I do something like checking up on our friends, too, but in a little different way. The point is that in our marriage we both have cared very much for others and have done something for others fairly regularly. Maybe some marriages don't last because they don't have their own interests, don't give the other space, or don't always get together as a family because they're too busy. Within some marriages one is very dominant, and when buttons get pressed, they don't know what to do. Dick and I had our own little routines, too. There were things we each could do. There was never a question about getting a divorce. If things were bad, you had to just put up with it. And when our family grew, Dick and I tried not to interfere in our family's lives. That came from our good marriage."

It seems as though Dick is still helping her as Bea plows forward, taking care of the home, cleaning out "stuff," listening to financial advisers, making important decisions, being supportive to Robin and Rick, and taking care of her own health. She rises early, is at the Y before 5:30 a.m., and follows a busy schedule that is at least half in service for others. The other half is getting together with her card-playing girlfriends and the Shipmates, visiting casinos occasionally, dining out with friends and family, keeping in touch with people, and just taking care of business.

Bea and Dick always had a good word for everyone and anyone they ran into. I liked their sense of humor and quick mirth. The couple had their share of health problems, and whether it was a treatment or surgery, they moved into the plan of the day immediately, never complaining. Their mantra might have been something like "Get up early, and get into the day", and "Be of service to others."

Dick Schantz passed away in April 2011.

Eileen and Bob Gluck
September 6, 1958

You do what you have to do.

In the mid-1950s, Eileen's and Bob's families lived in the Philadelphia area, in Springfield and Chester, respectively. They went to the same high school but were three years apart. Each took a little different track but did meet up in 1956.

It was summer in Springfield and Eileen Dear and her family had recently moved there. Eileen's mom and dad had married when they were thirty-four and forty-one years old and had her, an only child. Her mom had a stroke at the age of sixty-six and died, and her dad would live another ten years or so after that.

But that summer, one evening, she and two girlfriends decided to play miniature golf. Bob and two of his buddies also decided to play miniature golf at the same course.

Bob tells the story. "We happened to play behind three females whom we continually harassed and thought nothing of it until we got to the parking lot and found we were parked next to them and their 1956 brand-new Buick. It was one of the girl's father's…a policeman's car. A brand-new Buick. We all talked about the car and of course to each other. We asked where they lived, and Eileen said Springfield. Then one of the guys asked if they played cards and found that they played pinochle. So we all decided to go back to Eileen's house. They would drive, and we'd follow them. Well, we drove all around Springfield, and we boys thought the girls were trying to lose us. But we discovered Eileen was kind of new to the town and really didn't know where she was going. We finally got to her house, went into the basement, and played pinochle."

Bob was a student on a gymnastics scholarship at West Virginia, and when he was home on break over the Christmas holidays, he thought about calling Eileen.

"It was New Year's 1957," Bob said, "and I hadn't seen her since the previous summer, but I called and asked if she had a date. She did have a date, but we went out the next weekend. I think it was a movie, and we double-dated with one of my friends and his date from the neighborhood in Chester."

He returned to school and graduated the following May. Eileen had graduated from high school the year before and was working in downtown Philadelphia at the *Farm Journal* magazine as a secretary to the purchasing manager.

"I had signed up for the Marine Corps, but that wouldn't start until September so I went to work for the Ford Motor Company, the same place my dad worked and made seats for cars. I also dated a girl from college that summer."

In September, Bob went to Quantico, Virginia, where he had three months of boot camp. He got his commission as a second lieutenant in December 1957 and later was promoted to captain while in the reserves.

He said, "For the next nine months, I stayed at Quantico Weapons School, and during that time I called Eileen again."

"We dated during that time, and he came back and forth from Quantico to Springfield," she said. "Sometimes there were six marines making this trip back and forth."

"We went dancing a lot, and did some partying. One of my hangouts was the Polish American Club near Chester," said Bob. "Chester and Springfield were about twenty miles apart, and Quantico was another couple of hours."

"Bob proposed to me one night when we were out having a good time," said Eileen. "But I made him get down on his knees and propose a second time, because the first time we were out drinking and partying."

Quantico, on the banks of the Potomac River, was established in 1917 as a United States Marines barracks. A lot of World War I marines trained there. After that war it was established as a schools base. Higher-ups wanted to make it the Marine Corps Great University. Military strategies, techniques, and equipment were developed there. Bob became a first lieutenant and served four years. Semper fi.

"During the end of the Quantico time, we were to receive our orders. We thought stateside, but the orders stationed me on Okinawa. Eileen and I decided to get married in September 1958 before I would leave for overseas. It seemed to be a financially sound decision, relative to time."

Eileen said, "I was an only child, and my mother and I organized the wedding and the reception, which was at a local restaurant. My parents wouldn't pay for any alcohol, but plenty was bought for us from the cash bar. I wore a lovely white wedding dress, and Bob wore his marine dress whites."

Bob said, "My brother was in the navy, out to sea, and couldn't be in our wedding. He eventually became commander of a submarine; he was a naval academy graduate. I had four officers from my base as ushers, and one of Eileen's girlfriend's husband was our best man; he wore a nice tux. We were married at the First Presbyterian Church in Philadelphia."

"My best friend, JoAnn, was pregnant and, in those days, couldn't therefore stand up in the wedding, so another girlfriend, Pat, was my maid of honor, and Bob's sister Doris was a junior bridesmaid."

Bob said, "We had a beginning bond between us. The two people we wanted to stand up for us, my brother and her best friend, couldn't be in the wedding."

Bob and Eileen were married September 6, 1958, and left for an eighteen-day honeymoon. For the first night, Bob had made no reservations. They went to a hotel at the Philadelphia airport, and there were no rooms available. They drove on route 40 into Delaware and stayed at the Governor Prince Motel and had breakfast at Howard Johnson's the first morning.

"We just drove" Bob said. "We drove to Quantico to pick up pay records, some money, and medical records. We drove the Skyline Drive to Natural Bridge, Virginia, and drove through West Virginia and back through New Jersey and Pennsylvania. It was a motor trip. On the way home, we ran into a terrible rainstorm and had a flat tire. I was in a hurry to get to Eileen's home, because of a secret event about to take place."

"Well," said Eileen, "he pulled over and said, 'I have something to tell you.' And I said, 'Don't tell me we don't have a spare.' He said, 'No, we have a spare, but there's a surprise shower at your house for you tonight.'"

"I was a mess. I just wanted to get Eileen there on time and was happy to arrive finally and take a shower," shared Bob.

"Eileen's grandmother had a house at the shore in Ocean City, New Jersey, and when she passed, Eileen's family used it. We stayed there, near the boardwalk, for a few days. It was a really nice location. We were busy with a lot going on."

"I remember one time," Eileen added, "when we went to the movies. We saw *Lawrence of Arabia,* and Bob slept through it."

1958

This was a year of relative peace, as it was after World War II and the Korean War, and not yet Vietnam. Leading our country was President Eisenhower, and Richard Nixon was the vice-president...both Republicans. There was 4.3 percent unemployment and relative prosperity. Gas was a quarter a gallon, and a lady's dress, $3.98. The US *Nautilus* submarine passed under the North Pole ice cap, the micro-chip was invented, the Edsel was on the market (though not for long), and the Toyota first appeared for sale in the States. Our Supreme Court ruled that Little Rock, Arkansas, had to integrate their schools. The Hula-hoop was all the rage, with $100 million in sales that year. People listened to Elvis, who was drafted into the army, as well as Ricky Nelson, Frank Sinatra, and the Everly Brothers. They watched *Candid Camera, The Ed Sullivan Show, The Jack Benny Program,* and *Alfred Hitchcock Presents* on their TVs.

Bob went to Okinawa for fifteen months. He said, "Eileen stayed with her parents and continued to work in Philadelphia. The first Christmas was really hard. Even though we talked on a ham radio a few times, it was difficult. But we wrote letters weekly. I went to Hong Kong a couple of times after maneuvers in Borneo with the British navy preparing for Vietnam and bought some clothes for us. A cashmere coat for Eileen that our daughter still has. I also bought some suits and shirts and a nice dainty set of Noritake dishes, which we thought would be good forever."

His overseas tour was done, and there was a big reunion at the Philadelphia airport. They were stationed at New River, North Carolina, just outside of Camp Lejeune. They moved to base housing and bought some furniture.

"We also bought a nice little boxer dog and named her Ginger. Then we found out Eileen was pregnant; the baby was due in November of that year, 1960. I thought we should extend my service time in order to cover the baby's birth, and so we did that. We had our first child on the twenty-first of that month. We then moved in with Eileen's parents for a couple of months," said Bob.

"But," added Eileen, "we were able to buy a house a couple of months later. We moved to Ridley Park in Delaware County, and I stayed home raising Tammy, and then our second and third, Joyce and Stephen. We stayed there four years."

"I worked for Scott Paper, which later became Kimberly-Clark, in Chester, so we moved to Twin Oaks, which was closer to Chester. We were there less than a year when Eileen's mom died and her father didn't want to be alone," said Bob. "A transfer came up for us to move to Mobile, Alabama. Then we had two houses to sell: her parents' home and our home. We wanted to have the kids in school in September in Alabama so we were hustling. But the move never materialized, which I wasn't too happy about. We solved it all by selling both houses, buying another in Springfield, all moving into together, and I left Scott Paper. Our youngest daughter, Debbie, was born here in Springfield."

"That house was a nice split-level," said Eileen, "and our son Stephen lives in it now."

Bob continued, "Everything worked out well, actually. Sometimes it was a three-ring circus, because if someone needed help, we put them up. All family functions were held at our house."

"We put up a big table for holidays and special occasions by the fireplace, and everyone sat around it. At one time, Bob's sister lived with us. We were the center for the family," added Eileen.

"Our youngest daughter's girlfriend's parents moved to South Carolina, so she moved in with us for a while. Then, Eileen's dad died when he was eighty-four. He had lived with us for ten years," Bob said

"During that period, sometimes there were hard times. But Bob and I were always on the same page. When we were going through it, it was difficult, but afterward we knew we were OK," said Eileen.

With an inheritance from Eileen's dad, they bought another house in Ocean City, New Jersey. It was a duplex with good rental income, and they had it for twenty-five years. Eileen would go to the shore for the summer, and Bob would go down on weekends.

"Eileen started to get a little bored and wanted to get a job. That's when the shop Seaside Seven came into our lives. The owner also had a place near where we lived in Pennsylvania, so Eileen went to work in both places. Then the owner wanted to sell it, and we bought the Ocean City location," said Bob.

A Little Bit of History

Ocean City, New Jersey, is billed as a family-oriented resort on the ocean. It's as popular a place as you could find on the East Coast. Part of the barrier islands, the city has at least four access bridges to the approximately seven miles of sandy beach. It has been many things, from Indian fishing camps and cattle grazing areas to picnic grounds and a Christian retreat. But mainly it is, has been, and probably always will be home and a wonderful place to walk the boardwalk and vacation for a few hours or a few days. It was originally called Peck's Beach, named after a whaler who used it as his base. It has endured bad weather, fires, economic ups and downs, and most recently, pier damage from Hurricane Sandy in 2012.

It became a pastime, a departure from boredom, and a new interest for both Eileen and Bob. He was working at Crown Foundry as controller at the time. A client of a friend was interested in selling his gift shop, Drift In & Sea, also at the shore. And the Glucks were interested.

"We shook hands on the deal; everything was verbal and worked out well because both parties were truthful. So we ended up with two gift shops. Seaside Seven was more like a souvenir shop, and the other was more upscale, larger, and carried such items as pocketbooks, jewelry, collectibles (Hummels, Snow Babies, Annalee, Byers' Choice Carolers, Department 56 houses), paintings/pictures, Hagen-Renaker figurines, Christmas ornaments and decorations to name a few," said Bob.

Businesswoman Eileen ran both shops. But about ten years into the business, when Bob lost his job, Eileen hired him as her stock boy. They also had college students, home-town folks, and some efficient ladies working for them. Life was just plain busy. "I had one shop, and Bob had the other."

Bob said, "In the second store we had furniture and lamps, and we were among the first to get Thomas Kinkade paintings. We had a lot of stock and needed storage space, so we rented storage sheds off the island in Marmora. I'd drive a truck to move stock to one store or the other from storage, so I was always in transit."

Eileen added, "He was never where I wanted him. I was busy at one store, and he was doing work someplace else; we were always busy. One day I was trying to get an item from the rafters when someone came into the store and said to me, 'Why are you climbing the ladder?' and I said, 'Because I own the place.' You do what you have to do."

Over the years there were many obstacles, such as burglaries; teenagers fighting on the boardwalk, which resulted in broken front windows; and major damage and cleanup from a roof repair, including flooding and loss of inventory.

Doing business together for so many years seemed to be part of the good glue in the marriage. "Anything that came along, we just worked together at everything," said Bob.

"We had one of those stores for twenty years; the others, a shorter time. In 2002 we sold all of them. Eileen went away for the weekend to play cards, and when she came back, I had sold the last store. The new owner came and took everything we had, which was a really good thing."

"That's when we bought in south Florida and both retired."

Today, their four children are all married, and the Glucks have seven grandchildren.

Eileen said, "They have varied occupations, and we see them from time to time. Tammy, our oldest daughter, works at a food market and she and her husband, a retired machinist have no children. Joyce, our second born, recently moved from Florida to Texas and works for a teaching veterinarian. She and her husband, Paul, also have no children, and they travel a lot."

Bob said, "Steven, number three, works for UPS, driving tractor trailers. He and his wife have four children. His wife teaches preschool children and Debbie, our youngest, lives in Texas raising her three kids while her husband is a partner in a successful venture capital company. They get to travel frequently as a family.

"We bought in the south Florida community in 2002, were snowbirds until 2004, and then stayed permanently."

So, how about that...over fifty years married to each other!

Bob: We just work together at everything. Anything that comes along. Caring for her dad…raising our kids…working together in our businesses.

Eileen: You do what you have to do.

Bob: Before you know it, fifty years pass. We were very busy all the time.

For the past several months, Eileen has had health issues and sometimes feels unable to do many of the things she's been used to doing. She has been hospitalized periodically and continues to visit the doctor. Bob is healthy and is doing what is in front of him.

Eileen: Being sick as I am drives me crazy because I've never had nothing to do. But you know how your husband feels about you when you come home from the hospital and he says, 'Don't worry.' He does the cooking, the cleaning, and the shopping.

Bob: Our parents set good examples. I think we're setting a good example. You didn't leave…even if the other person is a pill; you stay together. Our folks all were very hardworking people, and that may have something to do with it.

Eileen: Most of our friends have stayed together. Our four kids all have stayed together; their in-laws have stayed together.

Bob: We blended together. I think people in a marriage know their duties, their roles.

Eileen: Sometimes I think a wife might have too much to say, and then the couple doesn't stay together. If it works for them, it's fine.

Bob: That means the husband has to stay strong. Having two strong people might be tough.

Bob: We're the opposite. I am strong, and Eileen isn't as much. We have arguments but move on to something else and don't stay there. Some couples fight all the time and over everything and give up, particularly in the celebrity circles. Sometimes the grass looks greener on the other side, and they cheat. Don't give up.

Eileen: Some have too much money and think they can afford to just leave or not be faithful. We have always been on the same page and always just do what we have to do.

Being business owners for many years, faced with much decision making and work, Eileen and Bob have always been on the same page. They continue that 'being on the same page' as they serve in many capacities for the worship service in their community as well as do service for others.

Peg and Tony Krawczyk
May 26, 1962

Roles and responsibilities within a marriage are well defined.

Tony's folks were Polish immigrants who settled in Lynn near other family members who had also come from Poland. It made for a lot of aunts and uncles. His mom had come from Krakow and his dad from Lublin. The area on the north shore of Massachusetts was typical of a lot of American cities where Europeans came to work and have a better life than what they may have had in Europe, early in the twentieth century. The city had its Italian area, Irish area, and Polish area. Tony went to St. Michael's Parish for church and school. His family had had a farm but lost it during the Depression and, like a lot of others, moved to a city.

"The beach was about a ten-minute walk," said Tony, "and we'd go there all summer long, every day. Every Monday, a friend and I took a cart to the beach. The county works took care of the beach, water supplies, and fireplaces.

People would picnic on weekends and leave their bottles. So we'd pick up the two-cent and nickel bottles and cart them to the neighborhood store, a Polish store. The other project we did on certain days when they were picking up the refuse. We'd go around and collect papers, iron, and tin, and when we had a load, we sold it to the junkman. We made a little more money that way; there were all different ways to make money. We were young kids and knew about the need for money.

"The neighborhood centered around sports, besides making money that is. During the day, when people were working at General Electric, their recreation field wasn't being used, so we'd climb the fence or burrow under it and play softball. They wouldn't chase us out. On the other side of the area was the town park."

Peg said, "Tony was an inner-city kid; and tennis wasn't one of his sports."

"I went to St. Michael's Polish school until the eighth grade," said Tony. "I was in a lot of plays, usually had the lead."

"He's not going to brag, but he's very smart," added Peggy.

"I had an older sister and we were going to go to school… me for the first time," Tony recalled. "I went in the front door and went right out the back door. My mom said, 'What are you doing? You're supposed to be in school.' School eventually was very pleasant. It was taught in Polish in the morning and English in the afternoon. Sister Michael in the fifth and eighth grades was very good and nice, as was Sister Angela. When it was time for the end-of-the-year tests, the sisters had copies of the past year's test so we could practice. It was a good system."

Working and making money with and for the family were as important as doing well in school. In the early twentieth century, immigrant families knew that learning English, being educated, and earning money for a better life was what it was all about for them in America.

"My parents worked, so in the summer we had to rotate who had to be home. I had one much younger sister and my turn to take care of my baby sister was in the mornings," said Tony.

Today, one rarely sees a kid on a bike, or pulling a wagon delivering newspapers. Back then, once a week, a newspaper kid stopped at your house to get the money you owed, and hopefully a little extra as a tip. Sometimes people avoided the newsboy and didn't pay for a while. Actually, now, one rarely sees a newspaper for sale in the afternoon. Back in the early and mid-twentieth century, those newspapers were the major form of extended news. Most towns had a morning and an afternoon newspaper usually published by different companies.

"I had a paper route in the afternoons; I had about four hundred to five hundred newspapers at two cents each. I had to be at the GE gate about two thirty in the afternoon to catch the people going into work, and a half hour later to catch the people coming out of work. I did half of my route, and more at four o'clock. Those were the war years of high employment, so a lot of people were going to work at all shifts. After supper I would hawk the papers in traffic.

"I lived in a neighborhood called McDougnah Square," said Tony. "We hung around the drugstores in the area. We would say, 'What do you want to do?' and we'd all just hang out together.

"During the war years of the 1940s," Tony said, "someone was always in line for bread, milk, potatoes, or meat. I remember the beginning of oleo…oleomargarine. There was an orange tab that you had to knead into the oleo to get the color of butter."

Many cities, including Lynn, had high schools that were different from each other. There would be one for students who planned or hoped to go on to college, one for those seeking vocational skills, and in some towns, one for business. Tony chose college preparatory.

"We had a ninth grade middle school, a grades ten-to-twelve school, Lynn English, and Lynn Classical. I had Spanish and took four years of Latin. We had a better education in parochial schools than in the public at that time," said Tony. "All my teachers said, 'You have to go to college.' My report cards were all good. An H stood for honors, and I did earn all Hs. One of the girls said, 'I can't figure Tony out. He has all these notes in his pockets.' What I did was get together with friends, cram, study for tests, and wrote notes to myself. I graduated high school but didn't go on to college at that time."

Peg added, "In his neighborhood he would be different because he was very bright; not everyone was. When he was in ninth grade, he was in a series of spelling bees and won, the *Boston Herald* Spelling Bee contest. I still have the paper on it."

"Well, I would have been a nerd in the neighborhood if I didn't play sports and be good at them," Tony said. "We played touch football, tackle football, baseball, and softball. I was one of the crowd."

A Little Bit of History

Lynn, Massachusetts, Tony's hometown, is about ten miles north of Boston and just north of the Saugus River with a population of about one hundred thousand people. It's an old industrial town, which began in the early 1600s as a tanning and shoemaking town. Two hundred years ago, it served as a suburb of Boston, and at one period in its history, twenty-three stagecoaches left the Lynn Hotel for Boston every day. In Tony's day, General Electric was organized to have both Lynn and Schenectady, New York, as home offices.

"I worked at General Electric and, after a year, enrolled in Salem Teachers College," said Tony.

Salem State was started in the mid-nineteenth century, one of Horace Mann's efforts toward teacher preparation. It was fifteen minutes from his home. Tony graduated fifth in his class and gave one of the commencement speeches. A few years ago, Salem State became a university.

Peg said, "I, on the other hand, grew up learning and playing all the sports. We lived in faculty housing on the campus of the University of Connecticut in the tiny town of Storrs." Storrs was named after the brother and sister who started the primarily agricultural school in 1881. Sixty years later the agriculture school became U Conn.

"My dad was a professor at the college, and it was a nice upbringing for me. All of us kids played on the regulation baseball fields when the college season was over; we all got tennis racquets one Christmas and played on the college courts. If they were locked, we'd climb over the fence. I babysat for the football coach, and we had free season tickets for football. Sports abounded, and I learned a lot of them at a young age.

"And, I, too, collected bottles for money. We'd take a wagon and go to the 'jungle.' The jungle was the men's dormitories. They would throw their Coke bottles out the window, and we would take them to the neighborhood store and trade them in for money. There was a fraternity at the end of our street, and the housemother would give us candy. We were faculty kids who were treated like pets. The fraternity back doors were close to our back door. I'd be out playing in the backyard and see college students who might have been drunk. I just knew it. Some of these areas were like the inner city. All of those things left a mark on me. I made up my mind I would always be in control of what I was doing."

Peg said, "By the time I was twelve, I knew there were problems in my home. My mom was an Episcopalian but brought the family up Catholic. I think some of our problems as youngsters were related to that. Tony's parents probably had an arranged marriage.

"In my junior year, my dad retired from teaching. We moved to East Hartford, and I lived with my grandparents. I went to a Catholic all-girls school where I learned more things about life. It's where I started smoking. Those girls were wilder than I was. It was an education, and looking back, U Conn was the hicks, an agricultural area. In East Hartford, we took the city bus to school. My mom was an elementary teacher. In my senior year, I talked some girls into painting 'Class of '56' on the parking lot, which was frowned upon greatly by the staff. The nuns were like black crows flapping around, trying to figure it out. No one knew who had done the whitewash job, but it was cleaned up very quickly.

"After high school I went to Boston University and found that a lot of students had come up from New York City, and most were of the Jewish faith. All my girlfriends were Jewish and wanted to fix me up. I said no and that I needed to date someone in my religion. My parents had made that point with me, to stay within the Catholic religion. It was funny later when I actually did meet Tony. I thought because of his last name that he was Polish and Jewish. When I found out he was Catholic, he didn't stand a chance!"

"I graduated and took a teaching job in East Hartford," said Peg.

"I graduated and took a teaching job in East Hartford," said Tony.

Education was important to the Tony, Polish-oriented city kid, as well as to the Peggy, the rural college-town kid. It continued to be important to them the rest of their lives.

"There was a beginning-of-the-year faculty picnic, and Tony and I met afterward at a pizza party," said Peg. "My friend Fran asked if anyone wanted to come down to his cottage at the beach on the weekend. Actually Tony had helped build Fran's place. My girlfriend and I said we'd go. On the weekend at Quonnie beach, there were maybe eight to ten people all having a good time."

Quonochontaug, known as Quonnie, Beach in Rhode Island is one of the many beautiful barrier beaches where mostly summer residents have lived since the early 1800s. It was a nice place to meet and get to know your future husband.

"That Saturday night everyone decided to go bowling. I had never bowled before, but Tony was there, and we talked a lot with each other. We took a walk on the beach and just went on talking. Later, I asked if anyone was going to the Catholic church in the morning, and Tony said he was. I asked him to knock on my door in the morning and get me up to go to church. When we parted company that weekend, I wondered if Tony had asked about me. He had."

Tony added, "She asked if I was interested in the big rivalry Yale–U Conn football game. I was. She had tickets. And she knew I bowled certain nights."

"As a result," Peg said, "I did join the bowling team. He didn't stand a chance. We went out a lot, but a few months later, the gym teacher asked me to go skiing. I said to Tony, 'What would you think if I went skiing with…,'and Tony said, 'If you go skiing, that's the end for us.'"

After Peg's first year of teaching, she transferred, taught kindergarten, and then taught third grade. "I loved teaching. I couldn't believe I was getting paid. Tony was going to be a lead teacher at the elementary level. Besides being good at his work, he was a very eligible bachelor, and our going out was the talk of the town."

Tony said, "Many people had previously tried to fix us up, and here we met on our own. We were ten years apart in age, met in September, and married in May—May 26, 1962."

"My principal asked me why I was getting married so soon, and I answered, 'I have to.' It was not to be taken the way it sounded. Actually Tony had a summer camp job. He was head of Duxbury and Camp Wing, and he needed to get there right at school's closing to set things up. We really wanted to get married before that and go there together."

"I had to get right down to camp," said Tony, "and after an Atlantic City weekend honeymoon, we left to prepare counselors and staff for camp."

"I can actually say I never had a second thought or a thing about him that I wanted to change," Peg shared. "I did tell my mom there was actually one thing I wanted to change. One thing: his socks. He would wear purple socks with a purple shirt or white socks with a suit. I told him that if he let me change his socks, I would polish his shoes once a week. I think I've actually done that once.

"It was an interesting summer. Tony was very busy and had little time off. I can say I got angry only once in our fifty-one years of marriage, and it was during that time."

Tony said, "I was going to take the night off, but there was an emergency and I had to stay for the meeting. Peg wasn't anywhere around."

"I was very upset because the one time we were going to be together, it didn't work that way. So I was mad and left in the car. I'm not that way really, am I, honey?"

"No, not since that time."

"I'm not that spoiled."

"We did go out some nights," Tony said. "The situation was resolved very quickly."

Peg asked, "Honestly, can you say that was the only time we were upset with each other?"

Tony smiled and agreed. Quite a record.

Over the years, Tony taught a fifth/sixth grade combo and junior high, served as head teacher, moved to half-time teaching and half-time vice principal, and eventually spent over a decade as principal at the elementary level. All in all, Tony spent thirty years in that role at different schools.

When he retired, he had 495 sick days turned back but could only get paid for about a quarter of them. That says something about his forty-three years in education.

Peg returned to teaching after being a stay-at-home mom with their four children. She taught prekindergarten, and then middle school reading and social studies for six or seven years. "We had four kids—boy, girl, boy, girl. We married in 1962, and the births were in sixty-four, sixty-five, sixty-seven, and seventy-two. I didn't return to teaching until the youngest was in school."

Peg and Tony talk about their marriage by generally describing the other. Peg said, "I knew he was a quiet man, not a partyier, and was religious. I think we take care of each other. I would never do anything to hurt his feelings or make him embarrassed. I would watch out for him if we were out socially. He could depend on me."

Tony added, "I never brought my problems home. When I left a school of four hundred kids and came home to a house of four kids, I didn't bring my work home."

"He gave his own kids total attention. He didn't talk about problems, so I just always thought he had a good day."

"Whatever we decided about taking care of the kids, we did together. I always backed her, and it was never a case of 'Why did you do that?' We never got into those discussions," he said.

"Tony is a very generous person. I know he would give me anything I ask for, but I'm not over demanding. As married with family, we put our children first. Both of us felt that our children were our treasures, our wealth, our jewels. We both still feel that way. If you're having a family, be on the same page; talk about it."

"Too many people may think that being married is being on a honeymoon," Tony added. "There are too many other things that you have to deal with and keep in balance."

"We worked very hard for the kids," said Peg. "All four of them went to private colleges, and from fifth grade on, all went to Catholic schools. We didn't have much extra. But I don't need new stuff all the time, and neither does Tony."

He said, "We never felt like we had to keep up with the Joneses and didn't have much money."

"Every picture of our living room over the years shows the same lamps," said Peg. "We kept things the same because there wasn't extra money, and it just wasn't important to us. As I said, the kids were most important to us. Do you know there were four kids in our home and there wasn't a ripple, no problems? I was actually concerned that they wouldn't recognize a problem."

I asked them, 'What do you say about marriage and how to make it to fifty years?'

Tony: You have to honor and respect your wife or husband. They're the most important person in your life.

Peg: Well, yes, put that person first, almost. Some men can't understand why a mother doesn't always put her spouse first. When you have babies and children, put your husband first, after, or alongside being a parent. Once you become a family, some men become upset if their wife doesn't give them everything. Tony understood.

Tony: Religion is important. It's good to have the same one. But, you can't really change others.

Peg: A lot of stuff that had certain responsibilities Tony took care of, and certain things I took care of. We each took responsibilities, and we trusted each other to do the job, that the responsibilities would be taken care of.

Basically, Tony went along with our child discipline, and we had the same feelings about child raising. Marriages can go awry if you're not on the same page with bringing up the kids. It makes for a lot of stress. I never said, "Wait till your father gets home." For example, we had tickets for the Boston Sox at Fenway. The two boys went to the top of a tree when their grandmother was babysitting. I told them to mind their grandmother. It didn't happen that day. So I told them that the tickets were going to someone else. But from then on, the kids showed respect for their grandmother.

I told the kids that I never wanted them to be called to the principal's office because it would embarrass their father who was a principal in our town.

We had a big get-together at the Outer Banks for our fiftieth anniversary. It was wonderful as nine of our twelve grandchildren and our four kids and their spouses were there. They sat down on a Thursday night, and our son started with "I want you to hear about my life." I realized that they did know what we were doing when we raised them. Each of our four talked about their relationships with us from camping to Saturday morning baseball card shopping.

Tony: You have to know your own self, and if you disagree, fine. Know your place and convictions in life. I don't like it when people say, "I don't want to get involved." I do want people to get involved. The less people speak up when there are problems, the more problems will exist.

Peg: You can never think you're going to change your spouse. Know yourself first.

Tony: You have to make sure of your own convictions. You know there are certain things you have to do; you can't avoid it.

Peg: I do think people wimp out in marriages. Some fail because they are misguided in thinking the other person will change, or, for example, they'll give up sports or stopping at the bar. You have to accept everything the way it is/was.

Tony: I think we saw too many things in our own lifetimes and decided that we wouldn't be that way.

Peg: Kids today see things in other families. They have seen the other side, but the time comes when they have to make up their mind as to what kind of life they want.

There's something about biting your tongue and maybe not being around certain people all the time, even if it's family.

Tony: Yes, you never live your life just to analyze it.

Peg: I like the idea of what you see is what you get.

Tony: It's been fifty-two years!

Peg and Tony do 'know thyself' and practice what they stand for. They do a lot of different sports and activities, speak their minds, live their convictions, and stand up for each other as well as the 'other guy'. They were totally involved in the health of their family as well as in any group they are in.

Hilda and Al Russell
January 28, 1961

Enjoy each other.

"**I** was working as a cashier in the PX at Bad Kreuznach near Mainz, Germany, and Al was a soldier in the United States Army. I sold him a bow tie...a bow tie with sparklers on it. We talked a little, and he asked me out for dinner. That was a little different from most GIs who often would ask girls out only for a drink," said Hilda. "I thought, well, why not? So I said yes. We made a date for a certain restaurant at noon, which was when a lot of us in Germany had our main meal."

"I thought she was pretty and looked forward to taking her out," said Al.

"Well, I went to the restaurant at noon and waited for him. He didn't come. I thought the heck with it; I'll eat by myself. So I did. I ate, paid for my dinner, and was ready to go, and here he came running."

Al explained, "I had a friend from America who came, and I couldn't leave him. I didn't want to be late but was. I offered to pay for her meal, and she let me."

"He asked me out again, and I wondered if I would just sit again. There was a river in town, and on the other side of it was a popular restaurant. We had something to eat—Russian eggs, which is potato salad with eggs. It was nice."

"Our first big, actual date, though, was when we went to Mainz, across the Rhine River, and Reudesheim, a famous wine town usually known as a romantic holiday town. We walked to the ferry and went across the river."

Hilda said, "Al bought me a white teddy bear and a box of German Linz chocolates. I carried the big teddy around all the time we were there. We stopped for a nice glass of wine and enjoyed the town. Well, we missed the last ferry going back. We tried to get a room for overnight, but no one would rent us one because when they saw it was a GI… well, you know what they thought. We stayed on a bench in a garden…a park. We kind of slept. I laid my head on his lap, and then we went for the first ferry at eight a.m. the next day. With a large teddy bear under my arm and at that time in the morning, I got some funny looks."

A Little Bit of History

Postwar Germany was occupied by a few different countries' armed forces. The US Army's Eighth Infantry Division occupied several different posts, one being Bad Kreuznach, which was southwest of Frankfurt. There were a lot of army installations in Germany. Al Russell of Rochester, New York, had been in Germany for several months when he met Hilda. He was soon to be discharged. World War II had ended a few years earlier in 1945, and the four major allied powers—the United States, England, Russia, and France—occupied Berlin and parts of the country. According to the Potsdam Conference, they were responsible for "denazification" and, at the same time, for helping the country rebuild and get back on its feet. It was a peaceful time, but hunger and poverty were everywhere. That occupation stopped in the 1950s, but a cold war prevailed between East and West Germany; the East was controlled by the Soviet Union, making that sector a puppet within the Soviet bloc. Germans living in East Berlin or East Germany mostly wanted out, either to West Germany or often to America. That was Hilda's route. In the United States, Harry S. Truman was president at the end of the war having succeeded the ailing and then late Franklin D. Roosevelt, with Dwight D. Eisenhower elected president in 1953. He had demonstrated powerful and popular leadership qualities as a four-star general and head of the European theater during the war. After Ike's two terms, John F. Kennedy was president for two short years, assassinated in 1963.

Al did return to the States and subsequently was discharged and settled in at a job, socializing and corresponding a little with Hilda.

"I also received letters from his friends, John and 'Little Al'," said Hilda.

"We wrote some, stayed in touch, but we were not really serious. The letters diminished. I was dating someone," Al added.

"I thought, 'I want to go to America.' If I didn't like it, I would come back."

One thing led to another, and through Al, Little Al sponsored Hilda to come to America.

"Hilda is coming to America next week," Little Al told Al one day. So Al stopped going out with the other woman and prepared to see Hilda. At the time, he was living with John and John's mother. There was space there, so they prepared a room for Hilda, which is where she lived, too.

"John's mother was Italian, nice, but very strict about how we all lived. Well, Al and I started seeing each other again, and it was nice. About a year later, Al asked me to marry him, I said yes, and we were married in the morning, at the end of January 1961, by the justice of the peace in Henrietta. Al's sister and her husband came, and we had cake and wine together," said Hilda.

The 1960s were good years to live in a suburb of Rochester, New York. Most people had jobs and were able to purchase a car or a home and usually both, and most people did not have big worries. Hilda and Al married on a wintry Thursday; the temperature was about eight degrees. Rochester had had twenty-five inches of snow in January alone.

Hilda had been trained in Germany to work with small animals and was on her way in the veterinary track. "But that became impossible to pursue in Germany, so I switched careers and became a hairdresser," she said. "And I worked at B. Forman's, a fine department store for a while, first downtown and then at Pittsford Plaza. I asked one of my customers, whose husband was a builder, if she knew of a place we could rent. She said her husband had a house to rent in Brighton, so for four years we paid seventy-five dollars a month rent. It was a nice house on Ashbourne."

"My foster mother was in real estate," said Al, "and she found a house that was for sale and was only ten years old at the time. I always wanted a basement, and the house at 560 Edgewood Avenue did have a basement. I looked at it, Hilda saw it, and we both liked it. So we put in an offer. We assumed the mortgage, paid the taxes, and moved right in. That was about forty-eight years ago."

1965

The year saw changes in the country. Vietnam was a conflict about to become a war. A year prior, race riots broke out downtown around Joseph Avenue, and fear remained in many people's minds and hearts. President John F. Kennedy, who was inaugurated in the same month that Hilda and Al married, had been assassinated two years earlier.

Brighton is a suburb of the city and has always been a charming little town on its own. Although Al and Hilda worked around and in the city, they returned after work to a lovely piece of country-like yard with a pleasing ranch home on it.

"There were apple orchards all around. The neighbors took good care of their grass and bushes, planted flowers, swept their walks, and were friendly with each other," recalled Al. "A nice place to live."

As Al said, he had to have that basement—first to do the creative work as he builds; second, to have a perfectly organized workshop to do repairs as he knows how to do it all; and third, to have a great party room. They have entertained in that special room many times. The party room is filled with fun places to play, including a "tilt" game, a jukebox, and a bar wrapped around an old piano.

"We spend a lot of time with eight couples, partying, picnicking, and traveling. But New Year's Eve is all about the party in our basement," said Al. "Since we bought the house, we've been having New Year's Eve parties here for at least twenty people, even thirty-two people. Everyone brings all kinds of good foods, and we have a variety of drinks. People bring kuchen, dips, sausage, potato salad, cakes, pies, wieners, and lots of hors d'oeuvres."

Hilda said, "Giving parties has been our hallmark. We've had masquerade parties, too. Everyone has a wonderful time, and they're all ages—mostly our age but some younger, too."

"We used to go once a year to Hamlin Beach State Park on Lake Ontario," said Al. "We'd go early and get many tables and a nice picnicking area. Everyone would bring good food, and lots of it. We'd eat and talk and play little games. It was always fun. The same crowd."

Added Hilda, "There are more than one German Oktoberfest in the area, but we mainly go to the one off Pinegrove by the lake. That's held for a couple of weekends in September, and we love it. The Krazy Firemen, the Spitze Band, and the Alpine Band, to name a few of the musicians, are there with German dancers and again wonderful food. We dance, talk, eat, drink, and watch. There's another fest in Spencerport and in Greece, besides some out of the area. We go with a bunch of friends."

"Over the years," said Al, "we've gone on sixteen cruises. We usually go with friends, and one time we went with a dear friend who celebrated his eightieth birthday. It's a lot of fun. We've traveled to Europe together, and Hilda's gone alone, too, to visit her sister and other family. The first time

Hilda and I went, Little Al went, too; that was in 1966 to Germany. We have traveled in Europe with her family, and sometimes we traveled without them. We've seen a lot of our country, too, most of the national parks. Once we took the train from Rochester all the way across the country to San Francisco and Los Angeles. Quite an experience."

"We were surprised when the state decided to run Interstate 590 right next door to us—I mean right next door," said Hilda.

Gone were the fields, the grass, and the trees to the north of them when five miles of concrete were poured from Brighton into the city. It followed what had been the former canal and then the Rochester subway bed. Several years later, huge concrete sound-barrier walls were erected, and they are still there.

"Every once in a great while, some motorist who has broken down on Interstate 590 climbs up the grassy hill, finds a little break in the wall, crosses the Edgewood bridge, and comes knocking on one of our neighborhood doors looking for help. Not so much anymore, as I guess most everyone has a cell phone," said Al.

Al worked for the Zute's Vending machine company and basically kept the machines filled and did the work required to keep customers happy. "We had to throw away everything that was in the vending machines after a certain date and replace with new. Usually the goods were still just fine. My neighbor next door for a long time loved chocolate and very often I'd deliver a bag of candies to her, supposedly for her grandkids, but I know she loved them.

"Zute retired his company, but I still wanted to work and liked the driving around the county. So I found a job delivering medical supplies, and now even though I'm almost eighty, I just love working a couple days a week. It gives Hilda time to herself, too. I will retire one of these days, but I'm not quite ready. I think it keeps me healthy. The only times I've been in hospitals are to visit people. That's not bragging; I'm just so grateful for good health. One time I was supposed to start walking and exercising more, so I joined the Jewish Community Center right up the street. That didn't last too long, and now I think the exercise of mowing and walking the lawn mower, plowing the driveway, weeding, carrying stuff, washing windows, and keeping the house and the garage and the trees in good shape is plenty. We'll see."

"I loved my hairdressing work," said Hilda. "Although I had received my licensing in Germany, I had to do it again here in America. So I did that. I met so many interesting people and so many nice ladies who kept in touch with me for years. I was with B. Forman's for twenty-one years, and after that I worked in a really nice salon right here in Pittsford. My customers and my boss were great and did nice things for me. I enjoyed knowing them. I retired and did just a few friends' hair for a while, but then I had cancer, and reaching up and holding the hairdryer was just too much for my arms, so that was that. I am a survivor though.

Hilda said, "We spend most all of our free time together. I think that is one of the main reasons we have been together for all these years; we really do enjoy each other.

"When we shop at the German market just over the border in Canada, or in Buffalo, or right here in the city, we love to buy wieners, smoked bratwurst, and the good candies. We used to buy at Heinmann-Hoffman's German market. Their sausage comes from Syracuse. Now it's Swan Market here. And, yes, we shop there together."

"Yes, we shop together," agreed Al, " but the exception is when you shop on QVC."

"Al spends time in the basement and the yard and does things for other families. He is very creative and makes surprise gifts for people."

"Hilda cooks really well; goulash, potato salad, all good stuff. She's the indoor person."

"When the casinos opened up within a short driving range," Hilda said. "Soon they offered a free room based on how often we went, I guess. They use the card that you slide, and every time points are recorded. Now we get a free room or two and an upgrade every several weeks. Our room is lovely and sometimes has a hot tub in it. One time the bed was so luxurious and high, I could've used a step stool to get into it. I was like a princess trying to get into her throne bed. We enjoy it very much. We win some and lose some. I think we've come out ahead but don't keep track. We have a good time going; it's a nice little vacation. Al and I really enjoy going there together.

"I've had some major health problems the last few years, and Al was always with me. I'd do the same for him. He is very healthy. We've had fifty-two nice years."

And how have you stayed married so long and so nicely?

"Most of our friends have been married fifty or more years, too. We have the same pastimes. We do compromise sometimes when needed," Al said.

"I never wonder, 'Why did I do this?'" Hilda added. "The time just goes by. Whatever we do, we do it with each other.

We just enjoy each other. We are pretty much relaxed as people. Most of our friends who have been married for a long time really like each other, too. When I was a child and some people were celebrating twenty-five years of marriage, I thought that was wonderful that they were still together."

Hilda said, "People don't stay together maybe because they insist on doing their own thing. You have to compromise. Some couples may stay together for the sake of children or because money is involved. Money can be a problem if it's spent on junk. And you cannot be selfish in a marriage." Al agreed and said the same thing.

"Enjoy each other while you can and as much as you can," said Hilda.

Neighbors of mine for twenty years, I have seen Hilda and Al at various times of the day and in various types of activities. They are consistently just plain nice and know themselves very well, and absolutely care for each other...and you and you and me.

Nancy and Sal Franco
March 25, 1972

There is no book of rules to follow; know that.

N ancy Lemke, born to Gus and Florence Lemke, grew up with three brothers. She was the baby. Sal, only child of Salvatore and Caroline Franco, went to parochial school. After their marriage to each other, they lived in Lake Grove, Long Island, for thirty years, then downsized and moved to Ridge. Eventually they sold everything, left the north, and settled in Florida.

Sal and Nancy look like they belong together. When meeting them, their faces are happy faces. Nancy has a quick laugh and Sal a rather constant smile. He comes to church early sometimes to greet the ladies with a good-morning kiss on the cheek. Nancy knows a lot of people in the community, and a lot of people greet her as a good friend. She is cute, athletic, plays ball, and is a really good tennis player. That's where we met, and it's to my advantage if I draw her as a partner. Sal is a student of learning, of the

Bible, of genealogy, and of baseball, particularly the Mets. They are class-A babysitters.

I get a kick out of their phone-answering voices: Sal has a peaceful "Gooood eee-ven-ing," and Nancy has what may be a Queens "Hallll-o." Each is his or her own person, yet for sure, connected.

1971

The seventies saw the progression of movements in our country—of individualism, environmentalism, feminism, and world peace. Republican Richard M. Nixon was our president. China was admitted to the United Nations, India and Pakistan had border fights, and gas was forty cents a gallon. World Disney Resorts opened in Florida, Apollo 15 astronauts rode a lunar rover on the moon, the price of an average new home was $25,000, and the first pocket calculator and soft contact lens were made public. The voting age was lowered to eighteen…that would be the twentieth amendment to the Constitution. A terrible upstate New York prison riot killed thirty-nine inmates and hostages at Attica. *Patton* won an Oscar over other nominees *Mash*, *Love Story*, *Airport*, and *Five Easy Pieces*; a ticket to see them was about $1.50. A favorite TV program was *The Partridge Family*. The seventies was still a decade of changes in our society, our economics, our global connections, and our lives. America was peaceful even though we were sending our troops abroad. The controversial Vietnam conflict continued until 1975.

"My wife had died in a car accident," said Sal. "It had been a good marriage." He had three children.

"And my husband had died in open heart surgery. We had a good marriage, too," Nancy said. She also had three children. "I was a little frightened as a single mom. I had a home, three kids, and a part-time job. It would've been hard.

"My brother had passed away during the same time frame, so my sister-in-law Rosemary, now also a widow, was going to a Parents Without Partners picnic and bringing her daughter. It was a winter picnic, held in December, and she encouraged me to go along. I did and brought my kids, too."

Belmont State Park is a lovely area in Babylon, Long Island, not far from their homes. In the warm seasons, you can go boating, picnicking, and paddle boating. Kids love it, even though you can't swim in the pretty little lake.

"We had a grill going with hot dogs and stuff. Everyone mingled. It was fun," said Nancy.

"I had made peanut butter and jelly sandwiches for my kids," Sal recalled.

"Pretty soon Sal and his kids came over. I think we had better food," offered Nancy. "And if I remember, he was flirting with other women."

They met, and that was that.

"The next time we met was at another PWP function, a wine-tasting party for adults only. It was over in Dix Hills, a little town on the island. Sal was there again," said Nancy. "We sat around and played a little pool. It was nice."

"I kept asking for her phone number. I had no way to get in touch with her, but Rosemary kept saying, 'Well, she'll be around,'" said Sal. "We said good night and left. No phone number.

"This is what happened to me the day of the wine tasting party. The minute I saw her walk down the stairs at the party, I knew she was the girl I was going to marry. You won't believe this, but here's what happened years ago, back in the 1920s. My father did the same thing with my mother. He came here from Italy, Sicily really, on a ship. He landed in Boston and was headed for Brooklyn because that's where his brother lived. He found the address and knocked on the door of the house, a two-story house. It was my mother who answered the door, as she lived there with her folks. Her sister Annie was married to my father's brother, and that was their home, too. Right then, my dad said the same thing to my mom: 'I'm going to marry you.' And he did. My mother told the story that same way but added, 'This cute little guy came up, and that's how we met.'"

Sal thought back to his pursuit of his first wife and said, "I've always been this way as far as really liking someone. I can tell if I like or dislike a person by the first impression, and 90 percent of the time, my first impression is right. I don't make friends easily, but I do so quickly and keep them for a long time."

Nancy added, "At Christmastime, I got a card from a girl I knew, and her last name was DeFranco. It reminded me of Sal having the last name Franco, and the card made me think that maybe he was going through the same thing I was. I knew he was a schoolteacher, widowed, and lived in Brentwood, so I called him. His mother-in-law answered the phone."

"Yes, that's right, my mother-in-law," said Sal. "She lived upstairs from me and my kids and wanted me to get married again. In fact, when my wife died…she wasn't even buried…my mother-in-law said, 'You have to get married.

You're one of these people who needs to get married. So don't hesitate; don't play around; just do it.' She kind of gave me her blessing right then and there."

"Well," said Nancy, "his mother-in-law answered the phone and must have known something about me, because she said, 'You won't believe this, but he's outside the Allstate Building looking for you. He's going to look at everyone leaving the building. He's there now.' Allstate was where I worked part time, and he was going to find me somehow. I guess when he came home from looking for me, she told him about my call. So Sal called me, and we went to McDonald's and just sat talking and talking.

"Same month, still December, and another friend called and said she was having a New Year's Eve party and asked if I wanted to go. I said, 'Loretta, who am I going to ask?' And she said, 'What about that new guy you just met?' I had told people at work that I met this really nice guy, but he was short and balding. A friend said, 'Grow up.' So I called Sal and asked if he wanted to go to the party. He said yes, and we've stuck together for forty years."

Sal and Nancy got together often from then on at his place or her place with all the kids. They spent almost all their nonworking time together. One time Nancy's son Michael, at age six, asked Sal, "Do you intend to marry my mother?" Sal said, "Of course."

"So," Nancy said, "three months later we were at Sal's house, and the kids were playing in the other room. He came over to me and said, 'Would you marry me?' There is no book of rules to follow. If there was, the book might say something like 'Are you sure you know what you're getting into? And you're going to stay home and raise how many?'"

Prior to that, Sal wanted to move in and just live together, and Nancy didn't because of all the kids. "The second time around, maybe all the bells and whistles don't go off, but I knew Sal would be a good father, and he was kind and good."

Sal gave Nancy his mother's ring. They set a date and were married March 25, 1972.

"We were married at St. Luke's in Brentwood, Long Island, and my father walked me down the aisle. Our best man was Bill Lombardi, and my brother's wife, Marilyn, was matron of honor. I wore a simple, high-collared long-sleeve, floor-length champagne-colored dress, and the girls all dressed in lavender. Sal and all the boys had tuxes. We had a reception for about a hundred people or so at the Half Penny Pub in Central Islip on Long Island. It was nice."

"The kids were ages ten, nine, eight, seven, six, and five years old. We had three girls and three boys, and we never were the Brady Bunch. After we were married, Sundays were interesting as we had three Catholics and three Lutherans, plus Sal and me."

Sal was hoping to take some of his high school students to Paris, and if so, he and Nancy would go there for a honeymoon. But not enough people signed up, so plans shifted, and they went to Curacao for Easter break and their honeymoon. Leaving six children at home required a plan, and both Nancy's mother and Sal's mother came and took care of them.

"It was work getting to know each other as we courted only three months," said Nancy. "If and when we argued, it was mainly over kids. Maybe one time there was a big fight…the Francos versus the Vacarros."

Sal added, "Right after we got married, we really never said to the six kids, call us a certain name. They called us Mom and Pop. They all got along, mostly. The kids were pretty accepting from the start."

A Little Bit of History

Lake Grove, where Sal and Nancy spent thirty years of their lives and raised their children, is a village in Suffolk County, Long Island, New York. It's about dead center east and west of the island, and about dead center north and south. Suffolk County is one of the state's larger counties with about one and a half million people and a fairly high cost of living. Lake Grove is a small village—maybe ten to twelve thousand residents—and an old one, settled in early 1700s along a former Native American footpath. It had a variety of names early on, but to honor the groves of trees in the area, Lake Grove became the official name. Farming, cutting ice, and eventually commerce was the way to make a living. There are a lot of state parks nearby and of course the beaches. It's a nice place to live and raise children.

"Sal had a house, and I had a house," said Nancy. "We should've sold both of our homes and bought a new house for us all. His mother-in-law, Dora, was dating someone, and she actually wanted to get married to this guy, Jim, and move out but really didn't want to leave Sal alone. When we got married, she did leave, and she, too, was married. We kept his house and rented it out. I had a brand-new home with four bedrooms and two baths. We added two more bedrooms. My kids kept the same schools and the same neighborhood. Our biggest mistake was having Sal's kids leave their schools and neighborhood. But we had a nice pool and a big yard, and it worked out.

"The children grew into their teen years. Some blended with the same friends, some liked sports, some wanted no part of sports, and some were really good students, but all basically got along.

"When our daughter Gina was born, Dora was her godmother. We always kept Jim and her in our lives," Nancy said. "Gina is about nine years younger than the youngest and is the glue between the two families."

Nancy and Sal are both dog people and always had dogs in the house, in addition to the nine people. Today they have a lightweight Chihuahua and once in a while dog-sit for family.

"I was academically inclined and expected more from my kids," said Sal. "One of our daughters didn't like school and married young. I told her and her husband, Joe, that they'd have to work their problems out whatever they might be. Well, they did. Now married thirty years, she has her master's degree and is a schoolteacher."

Sal, who was a French and Spanish teacher at Seaford High School, had a typical teacher's salary when they first were married. He tutored and did summer work, too. Later, even though the annual income had increased, that one salary had to go a lot further.

"Finances were very difficult when we first got married. Nine people. Hard to save anything. But I can't remember any fights over finances," said Nancy. "We talk about everything. We don't do anything major without a lot of communication, a lot of talk, whether it's buying a five-hundred-dollar TV or a car or a house. There's never a lack of communication. Neither one of us would make a major move of any kind without the other person. We always talk about it, on the level with each other."

"I did an Idita-Walk, a virtual 1,049-mile walk across Alaska, and recorded it on the computer," Sal said. "It's from Nome, Alaska, and one minute of walking counted as one mile. I bought a seventeen-dollar T-shirt online commemorating the occasion of reaching my goal. Before purchasing, I asked Nancy if it was OK to buy the shirt."

Nancy added, "I said, of course. I think sometimes there are people out there who do decide to just buy something without discussing it. We are constantly talking to each other.

"During the summer, when school was out," she said, "we bought a camper and took the kids camping. The first year we had rented a popup and went around the state and stayed all over with no itinerary. We did it by the seat of our pants. It rained the first nine days of a two-week vacation. So when we first set up, Sal said, 'Don't touch the tent while it's wet.' I, of course, did. It leaked. The kids enjoyed it the first time, and they enjoyed it even more when we had our own trailer and went around and camped."

They decided to go away alone, too. "We needed that," they agreed, "and we stuck to that plan for quite a few years."

For one of those getaways, a schoolteacher friend and his wife volunteered to watch the kids. It was an example of family pulling together as the babysitters, and the young teens didn't quite get along. The kids basically tried to ignore the adult babysitters, banded and bonded together, and watched out for each other. Dora came over as relief and watched the kids.

"Sal and I pulled together when one of our kids had some difficulties, and Sal could've walked away. He didn't," Nancy said. "All seven children are basically independent. Sal and I didn't always agree about raising kid. Most of the arguments were over the kids, basically one of his and one of mine. It crossed my mind that we're still fighting over them at times. A while ago, I stopped and thought. I realized that it's not really about the kids; it's about us. Counseling may or may not have helped; we went a couple of times. Our marriage, sometimes, could have gone either way. It wasn't easy blending the family. It's easier to walk away from a marriage when things get rough, but you have to stick it out.

"We went to a marriage encounter weekend, and we came out of it on a real high. It makes you think of the stuff you liked about your spouse in the first place."

Marriage the second time around with so many children and tight finances set the stage for some difficulties. But this is what I heard from a winning couple who celebrated over forty years of marriage.

How have you made a long-term marriage work?

Sal: Marriage is work. Maybe sometimes one person has to give in more than the other. I mean, someone does. In our marriage, it's probably me that gives in more.

Nancy: I have to admit, I'm the mouth in our marriage. At times we do holler at each other; it's half joking. We don't do much of that, only when we have to. After we got married, I held back a little bit in hugging because I didn't want to show affection for his kids in front of my own kids.

Sal: I hugged them all, most all.

Nancy: Watch out for expectations of each other or of the kids. Look at your expectations; don't have too many, or too high.

Sal: You try to be fair. It took me a lot of years to figure out that you can't be totally fair.

Nancy: We have never used the word "step...someone" or "half-sister" and or anything like that.

Sal: A kid can put a damper on a marriage; sometimes it can make parents go at each other. Recognize it when and if it happens. Keep it together, and try to be on the same page.

Nancy: Do not let a child destroy what you have between the adults. Deal with the problem, and deal with the kid, of course, but remember that you and your spouse love each other.

Nancy: Just don't argue over money.

Sal: Stick it out.

Sal: We really looked forward to going to Paris. But go with the flow, as we did when the Paris plans didn't materialize; there was a plan B.

Nancy: Get away alone from your family for a little vacation.

Sal: When your kids have a problem, tell them to work it out. We haven't always done that with every kid but we have been there to help, too. It depends upon the circumstances. But usually, let them do it.

Sal: If there's tough stuff, maybe see a counselor or do marriage therapy for a bit. Sometimes it works, and sometimes you don't know if it does. But make use of talking to someone outside the marriage.

Nancy: Communication is key. Talk about everything all the time.

Nancy: Remember that you and your spouse love each other and talk, talk, talk.

The girl from Queens and the boy from Brooklyn tell me that marriage is an everyday thing. Recognize your need to get married if that's the case: know thyself, as Nancy knew Sal would be a kind and good father to her kids. She recognized her own concerns about herself as a single mom as well. Sal also knew himself; early on he knew Nancy was the one for him. It's a romantic story the second time around.

Pat and Carl Foucht
September 22, 1962

Having similar views on social and political issues worked well for us.

"It was either the Young Republicans Club or Young Professionals in the early sixties where we met. They had singles' events and called them 'Bachelors and Bachelorettes.' I'd go with the girls, and a bunch of us would go to the different events. We'd dance, have a drink, and meet new people. The events were held at various places like the University Club, the Trenholm Inn, nice places mostly downtown, and guys would ask us to dance. One night Carl came over and asked me to dance. He took my phone number, and I thought he'll be like a lot of guys who just ask for phone numbers," said Pat.

"I still have the little black book, and I still have Pat's telephone number in it," Carl added.

"Well, he did call. Carl was going to the University of Rochester part time and used to go up to Crittenden and

Mt. Hope, where there was a drinking and meeting place for young people," continued Pat.

"We'd go there Wednesday nights. I'd pick her up, as Pat lived nearby. We enjoyed talking with each other."

"When Carl was in Boston, he was dating a girl, and I had been dating a high school sweetheart for a long time."

During their first meeting as unattached singles, they really enjoyed conversation with one another and soon became a couple and later got engaged.

The Atomic Energy Project, which existed from 1943 to 1971 at the University of Rochester and where Pat worked briefly, was shut down because some thought the oversight was not rigorous enough as related to radioactivity. Their job was to develop and monitor peacetime atomic usage. They have recently contacted Pat as a former employee regarding any health issues.

"Pat was working for the Atomic Energy Project at the hospital as part of the U of R and wasn't really happy with it. She'd get run down as a result of it, so one day I suggested, 'Go out and get another job.' She went from bank to bank downtown, and Marine Midtown Bank was looking for a secretary to the comptroller," said Carl.

"Well, the comptroller was going to night school just as Carl was. When I interviewed, I said, 'I am engaged, but my husband-to-be is going to night school for his MBA, and we are going to wait to start a family.' The employer appreciated my honesty, and so I started right then. The assistant comptroller was nice. I actually found time to type some of his kids' school stuff as well as Carl's term papers."

Political groups for young adults have been around since the mid-nineteenth century. The Young Republicans started in New York City in 1911 and is the oldest in our country. They still exist today as meet-ups and social networks. When Carl and Pat were members, the clubs were not only for social gatherings but also a place to hear speakers on issues and a starting point into politics. Republicans traditionally have been conservative but do have a liberal faction. One of the stronger conservative Republicans of the day was Barry Goldwater, a US senator from Arizona.

"Pat's father was conservative, and we became active in the Conservative political party. We were big fans of Barry Goldwater and were very active. One time we went to Buffalo to hear him."

"My father," said Pat, "was in business and did not like any government over involvement." That was a Republican stance.

"And," Carl added, "my family members were mainly teachers and farmers, and in a way, paid by the government, so they wanted the government to stay involved." That was a Democrat thing.

Issues are important to Carl and Pat and being informed has always been part of their way of life.

1960s

In the '60s, political and social thinking was becoming more liberal. Government became stronger in our lives, and our population seemed OK with that. Laws were passed granting equal pay for both sexes; racial integration was furthered and challenged; and government pushed ahead with nuclear and outer space exploration, often with little disagreement. Government controlling more of our lives was a Democrat attribute. Times were changing. Firsts were everywhere: Kennedy was our first Catholic president, and in Rochester, New York, Henry Gillette, the first Italian mayor, was elected. Dr. Martin Luther King Jr. was arrested again, as he led peaceful marches for black Americans to be treated as equals. National treasury money was spent on space exploration as John Glenn orbited the earth, and our military strength was furthered with the establishment of the now famous US Navy SEALs. The sixties were a time of philosophical changes. Carl and Pat were thinkers and principled people.

"We went to Ohio to meet Carl's family. Carl's dad had passed away, and his mother left the farm and moved in with his grandmother. When his grandmother met me, she said, 'Well, you're a tall one.' I guess that was good."

Carl said, "My mother was reserved."

"You are more like your mother," replied Pat.

He agreed. "Most of my family was that way."

Carl had been brought up in central Ohio, and came from a farming and teaching family. His great-great-grandfather had purchased about 160 acres of farmland in the 1830s, and there, generations of Fouchts worked and resided. At last count, there were maybe 175 people who lived in his hometown, which has not changed much.

Pat grew up in Rochester, graduating from James Monroe High School.

At the time Rochester City School District was well regarded and successful. According to the 1950 demographics, the population was about 97-plus percent white and 2-plus percent black. Today, it's about 41 percent white, 41 percent black, and the rest Asian and Hispanic. And the school district is failing. James Monroe High was a lovely stone and brick school built in 1923; that would make it ninety years old now.

"I was a pretty strong Republican back in the Nixon days. Nixon and later Reagan were allies of Goldwater. I was raised in a Democrat family, so we would get into pretty interesting discussions with my family," said Carl. "I kind of think in a marriage if a couple doesn't think along the same political lines, it could cause great problems. I would think it would be very difficult. If I had been a liberal when we first met, Pat, your family wouldn't have like it."

Carl worked at Delco, and Pat worked at the bank. In addition to her day job, Pat was a dancer. She had taken ballet and taught it and ballroom. "I went to Arthur Murray Dance Studio, and it happened that my instructor asked if I could go to work with him. His name was Harry. He would come over to my place, and we'd work on dance steps. Then I'd go out at night and teach dancing with his brother after working all day. I loved it. Carl took some lessons, too. When I was going to get married, a girlfriend said, 'You can't teach ballroom after you're married.' I agreed, as that was the kind of thinking we had back in the sixties. It's entirely different now. If I did go back to teaching now, I'd have to relearn."

Carl added, "She even taught the president of Canandaigua National Bank in a dancing class."

A Little Bit of History

Born in Galicia in 1912, Arthur Murray marketed dance step diagrams and taught dancing by mail. He purchased a few TV spots in 1950, and his wife, Kathryn, showed dance steps. Two years later he televised the *Arthur Murray Dance Party* and eventually franchised dance studios that still teach the fox trot, the waltz, swing, and more.

Delco, part of General Motors, was Carl's main place of employment for about thirty years. North East Electric Company of Rochester (circa 1908) was purchased by GM in 1929 and eventually through the years made windshield wipers, and motors for adjustable seats and electric window activators. During the war, the three shifts turned to making electrical parts for warplanes and machine guns. The original location on Lyell Avenue was close to the subway, but it was eventually vacated for a new plant farther out on the same street. In the last decade, numerous fires and vandalism have befallen the original building. Delco as it once was is no longer.

Carl was devoted to General Motors, and he was well respected by all. He never looked around for greener pastures. This, too, was characteristic of Carl and Pat.

"I was happy with industrial engineering at Delco. I did a short stint in production control and didn't really enjoy that. Pat said I used to come home crabby. It was a different type of work, dealing with day-to-day stuff. It wasn't long-range planning, which I liked. So I went back to industrial engineering and loved it."

"The environment was good for you," added Pat.

He had to activate the change himself aggressively. Carl said, "One night I was working until about seven p.m., and I wondered if my boss, Ron, was in his office. He was, and I dropped in. I asked about the supervisory job I used to have and said I just wanted him to know that if someone was leaving and the job was open, I'd throw my hat in the ring. The boss showed some interest, and, well, I got the job back. That was great. I stayed there until I retired."

Pat said, "You were so happy."

"I really had a wonderful career at Delco, met a lot of good men. When I approached the age of fifty-five, I wasn't ready to leave Delco, but it was what it was. I thought I'd try what my sailing friend Tom was doing: working at a temp agency. I worked for Xerox for a few months and it was fun." Then he turned his head toward retirement and other adventures.

"Sometimes I wish I'd had a career besides raising the kids," Pat said. "I did find a part-time job working for a pediatric dentist. The boss was great, and it was a nice job. Would have been nice to have had a career, too."

Pat and Carl married a few months after their engagement on September 22, 1962. It was a lovely wedding, and the reception was held at the Valley Echo Club. Pat wore a stunning long white gown and Carl, a tux. They settled in the suburb of Brighton and soon had two children, Cheryl and Craig. Both children were born premature. Cheryl had actually weighed one pound, 13 ounces before she came home. Both children were healthy and grew well.

They decided to move a little farther out...in the country. "I wasn't too happy with suburbia. Seemed a little materialistic,"

Carl said. One evening after work, he drove Pat out to Victor, up Strong Road, and showed her some land.

Pat said, "We drove down this dirt road, and there was a big field."

Carl asked, "Pat, could you live here?" She could, they did, and they do still. They built a roomy Cape Cod and landscaped the property beautifully. They composted and grew vegetables and planted a ton of evergreen trees. Both have a love for the outdoors and for animals. Her dad had a "farmette" in the area, and as mentioned, Carl grew up on a farm.

Pat said, "We've been here in the wilderness for forty years, and we love it."

The children went to Victor schools and enjoyed other activities, too. When Craig was on the Victor swim team, Carl was a referee. Cheryl was a swimmer, too. Both went on to college, and they visit fairly often. They are close to each other and think the world of each other.

"The kids are happy for and with each other, and we love them," said Pat.

"We were married in the Lutheran Church and are Lutherans today. We have become allied with the Evangelical Lutherans. There is a difference in beliefs among Lutherans, and it all is according to the synod you belong to," explained Pat. "There is the Missouri Synod, which we're not part of. It interprets the Bible very strictly; for instance, they don't believe in ordaining women. They are the LCMS. We are part of the ELCA, which believes in interpreting the Bible a little differently, a little more ecumenically, especially concerning Communion. There is a third faction, too…the Wisconsin Evangelics."

"But," added Carl, "we made the decision together after understanding the various interpretations of the Bible. We are members of the Lutheran Atonement Church in Brighton."

"Pat's father had become involved in owning some real estate, and it looked like a good thing for us to do," said Carl. They talked it over, did the pencil-and-paper thing, and before they knew it, they were landlords for several multifamily homes in the city.

"Early on I got to thinking what kind of activity would be good for the family," said Carl. "I golfed a little at first, and then I thought Pat would become kind of a golf widow if I continued. I was never involved with football or baseball, sports like that. I didn't have interest in those sports. I thought, 'Sailing is something you can do with your wife and your kids.' So I got my first sailboat after Tom Grape and Ralph Edwards took me sailing with them and I enjoyed it. I went sailing a lot with Ralph down at the Canoe Club in Irondequoit Bay. Pat always crewed with me."

"We all took lessons, and we all enjoyed it," Pat confirmed. "We'd go on the sailboat together. We have a friend who said she had to become a sailor if she wanted to be with her husband. It is a pastime that is good for families."

"The Thistle, a nice-day centerboard sailer, was our first boat," Carl said. "Then we got the Ensign, which was more stable. We sailed that until 2000 when we sold it. Now I crew with a group on an Ensign, and Pat crews with another group on an Ensign. It's kind of nice, actually—no work on the boat, just show up and sail. Over all, we had boats for about thirty years. Craig and Cheryl were OK with it; they weren't wild over it but did it. They don't sail now though. It takes four people to crew the Ensign, and that worked out for our family."

"One time," Pat recalled, "we were out, and it started storming. We were taking on all this water, and Craig leaned over and said to me, 'Mom, we're fine. Don't worry. Don't get upset.' The decks were awash, and I was a little worried. I thought that was good of Craig.

"We joined the Canandaigua Yacht Club along about the time we got our boat and had a good time there. Carl was commodore for a bit, and we all enjoyed going there."

"I sail now only to race," added Carl.

A Little Bit of History

In 1891, the Canandaigua Sailing Club was formed with eight members. Its clubhouse was a hut on a flatboat off the city pier, and dues were five dollars a year. A little different from the Canandaigua Yacht Club that Carl and Pat joined.

"On one occasion, we went bare boating. We rented a large boat for ten days and sailed in the Virgin Islands area. You do your own sailing, and the first time we did it with two other couples from the yacht club. There were probably eight to ten boats with other members on them. We'd anchor and visit with each other A few years later, there were two couples at church who also had kids, friends of our kids. One of them partnered up with another couple with kids so there were eight of us on a fifty-foot boat. It was a lot of fun. We went snorkeling, and all the kids got along. Boating has been good for us as a family as well as for the two of us," said Pat.

A medical situation out of the blue, as most medical situations are wont to do, arose, and Pat and Carl discussed, researched and made their decisions.

"I think the breast cancer was a shock," said Carl.

"The question for us," Pat said, "was mastectomy versus lumpectomy. I didn't know."

Carl replied, "I used to go on the computer and do research and read about different drugs and studies."

"The breast coalition talks about all phases of breast cancer."

Pat and Carl are active and enthusiastic members of the Breast Cancer Coalition. It was formed in 1997 in Rochester and is part of the National Breast Cancer Coalition as well as the state organization. It is full of information and support and people. There are events such as the Pink Ribbon Walk and the 'ARTrageous Affair', free programs, support groups, book clubs, and brown-bag Fridays..

"I've had one doctor ask me why I had a mastectomy. Some can't take this. It can even be a problem in a marriage," explained Pat.

"It was ultimately our decision," Carl said.

"We were able to discuss what I should do. I did ask the doctor, but it was Carl's and my decision. It stays in your mind and goes through your head all the time. Any ache or pain I think…that's it. There are no guarantees. You learn to live with it.

"With cancer, they're always looking for recurrence," she says. "Doctors want to check."

"I've supported her in the breast cancer; in the activities. I've always been involved in the Breast Cancer Coalition. My main function is being a bartender during the social event where the art for sale is shown."

I asked them why they thought some couples couldn't stay together.

Carl said, "If people don't have common interests, it could be difficult."

"Or if they have major disagreements on how to raise kids or disagree about politics, that could make it difficult to stay together," said Pat.

Pat and Carl talk, and they agree. Carl said he thought it must be difficult for a couple if they disagreed politically. Many couples don't even have an opinion about issues or politics. Pat and Carl do. Together they changed their conservative views totally around to a liberal interpretation for government, because each of them didn't think the Republicans were addressing some of the issues squarely. So now they are liberal Democrats.

Issues of any level of government, church law, society, minorities, health, ethics and finance have been of interest to Carl and Pat. Standing up for similar beliefs and causes, making decisions after thorough communication and choosing common activities for family, all contributed to a happy and long marriage.

Joan and Chuck Van Velson
June 27, 1953

Have a good share of tolerance.

"I was a bridesmaid in my friend's wedding, and Chuck's brother was an usher. I think Charles may have had nothing better to do and decided he'd go to the reception. There we met. He said he liked my brown eyes and the way I looked. I was skinny back then. We danced almost the whole night together. Well, my dad said to a friend nearby, 'Someone should break that up; I don't want my daughter with that old man.' Actually I was twenty, and Chuck was twenty-seven," Joan said.

After high school, Joan enrolled in and lived at the Helen Wood Nursing School, part of the University of Rochester, and that was where Chuck picked her up for their first date. They had pasta at a restaurant nearby. Chuck was dating two other girls at the same time, but soon they were exclusive.

"When I was in nursing school," Joan said, "I had to be in the dorm by ten p.m., and one a.m. on the weekend. Too bad there aren't those kinds of restrictions in place now... probably would help. I don't agree with what's going on with that age group; it seems there aren't enough restrictions because someone always thinks they're being stepped on."

"One time, while still at Helen Wood, I rode my bike from the dorm to Arnett Boulevard where my sister lived with her husband. I called Chuck up and asked him to come to dinner. He came over and then drove me home to Delmar Road in Greece. I left my bike and was to get it later. Chuck pulled into our driveway, and my dad yelled at him, 'You're too old to date my daughter,' and then my mother said the same thing. I wanted to leave and told Chuck to take me back to my sister's. He said, 'No, you stay here and straighten it out.' So I did go into my house and spoke up in my defense."

Joan's parents had a difficult time with the age difference. That was the early 1950s.

"Well, I quit nursing and started working at Hickok's in the personnel office. Chuck worked at Kodak's Camera Works downtown and later at the Kodak Elmgrove Plant. We dated that year, and the following year we were engaged—in April of 1953. Chuck had enlisted in the navy when he was seventeen years old during World War II. He got out when the war was done but was called back for the Korean conflict.

"We were downtown one time before Christmas, and he bought me a set of rhinestones from Hensler Jewelry. I still have it. Later, at another time, we were at a jewelry store in the Temple Building. We window-shopped, and before I knew it, we had picked out my engagement ring. We were engaged right there. He was romantic, yet he wasn't romantic. That was April eighteenth, and now I have that diamond in a necklace."

Joan's family was Catholic, and Chuck's parents were active members of Bethany Presbyterian Church. In fact, when Joan attended Holy Cross, she had the highest marks in religion. So, like the age thing, this was another issue. It was the early 1950s, and parents usually didn't like their daughter or son to marry outside of their faith.

"I didn't even know if my dad would walk me down the aisle or not. We were married at Bethany. I think we were the second couple to be married there in the new church by the Reverend Alfred Wangman. My parents did come to the wedding and didn't stay for the reception. The reception was at St. Paul's Exempt, and it was nice. My brother and two sisters were there with their families. One sister was a bridesmaid and the other my matron of honor."

1953

1953 was a good year in the United States, and in Greece, New York, too. There had been eight years of postwar growth in our country and relatively peaceful foreign relations, and the Korean armistice was signed. Little did we know that those few years were the last few in a row without conflicts. Starting a marriage, a home, and a family in the mid fifties in the United States was a good thing. Stamps were three cents, and unemployment was 3 percent. There were no huge issues that affected suburbanites, or most city dwellers either. The world was interested in Queen Elizabeth II's coronation and the first scaling of Mt. Everest by Edmund Hillary and Tenzing Norgay. America's headlines were about the first open heart operation performed in Philadelphia, the Yankees versus the Dodgers, and golf champions Ben Hogan and Patty Berg. Money stretched and middle-class folks could think "investment."

"By the time Ellen, our first, was born, we all got along just fine. We were all very good together. My parents came over to visit often, to help out, and also to play pinochle. My mom and I played against Chuck and Daddy. I was a stay-at-home mom most of the time. Then we were pregnant with Kathryn, and for a little while I worked part time. Chuck's mom came over and babysat Ellen. But I was home most of the time. Between Kathy and Keith, I worked a shift at Hickok, the St. Paul Street location, from six to eleven p.m. Chuck babysat. It was good for both of us. I stayed home until Keith was in grade school and worked a part-time schedule around the children. I never worked full time. First I had a job at Edwards Department Store in Ridgemont shopping mall and then DC Turner where my sister worked. I got a job there starting at about nine in the morning until three thirty a few days a week. They eventually went out of business though. My friend Norma told me about micrographics. She was a secretary at a church, and her friend Bud had a small print shop. So then I worked part time in his printing business. For a while my mother lived with us. When Bud moved his shop to another location, I went, too, doing typesetting. Actually I did a lot of troubleshooting for that agency.

"Then another friend, Gail, whom I met in a downhill skiing and snowmobile club told me about a job at the *Penny Saver* newspaper. I ended up working there twenty-two years part time, and it was right in Greece. When Chuck was in his mid fifties, Kodak decided it was going to bring computers in, and he and others would have a lot of retraining and new learning. Kodak had given us a good living, but at the time nothing was uniform in the financial settlement for the people who retired or left. Some got a year's severance, some guys got nothing, and some got the bridge. Chuck decided at that time…he was fifty-seven…that was it. Time to leave. He received a few months' severance pay, but there was no Social Security pay until he was sixty-two. So that *Penny Saver* job helped Chuck and me through some lean financial times. I don't feel sorry for all those who lost their dental insurance lately, for example. We always worked it out though and hung tough.

A Little Bit of History

The town of Greece goes way back to the Algonquin, Iroquois, and Seneca days along Lake Ontario's shore and up, down, and around the Genesee River. French and then English/American settlers came, and in 1792 the first permanent settlement was created on the west riverbanks. That would be near the area where Joan and Chuck grew up and lived all of their lives. There is a little neck of the city of Rochester reaching between the river and Greece called Charlotte (Sha-LOTT), and that is where they went to high school. Down the riverside is where Kodak established its first plant in 1891 and where Chuck worked his entire life. Greece extends just north of the ridge, which is a topographical feature that the weather markedly changes, and that ridge is eight miles south of one of the Great Lakes. Lake Ontario and its sandy beach are a few yards from where they have made their home for fifty years or so. Their golf club, church, workplace, bridge clubs, and senior center are all within a few miles. Today, Greece is a town of ninety-five thousand people but wasn't always so. The Van Velsons and the Spragues grew with it. Almost everything they did was not far from home.

Joan and Chuck liked activity and particularly sports. They were Greece/Charlotte kids, and their world consisted of places to go in that northwest quadrant of the county. Chuck had always said he wouldn't join a country club until he retired, but in 1983 they joined Deerfield Country Club. It was an era when many new clubs were starting up with golf and usually a social aspect, all affordable.

"I talked him into playing in a husband-and-wife golf tournament at Deerfield. We were on the sixteenth hole, in front of the green in two, and Chuck hit the next shot into the woods. I called him a not-so-nice name in jest, and he reminded me of that until his dying day. We ended up winning it actually. We played with others and won different tournaments over the years."

Joan and Chuck played a lot of golf and in 1992 started playing at Lakeshore Country Club, just down the street from their home. Chuck wasn't wild about tournaments, and for a long time, he played eighteen holes five days a week. Later he switched to nine.

"I played in a lot of tournaments with other women and met some opponents who were fun and some who were not so gracious. Chuck and I played with a few really close couples and socialized a lot."

Joan's name was on the Rochester *Democrat & Chronicle* sports page frequently as winning or placing in a golf tournament, usually at Lakeshore country Club. She won the Senior Club Championship once, and Low Net another time. It seemed as she won one tournament or another every year.

"We did have a boat for a period of time. The first was a sixteen-foot motorboat, and we trailed it to Ontario and rented a cottage on Canandaigua Lake. I remember when we first were there…Keith was in kindergarten, and the girls were nine and eleven. Chuck got the boat secured and, because he had a tough migraine, went to bed. The kids went down to the pier. Keith was about to jump in the lake, and his toe got caught in a looped rope. We ended up in emergency with that injury. Another time, during the night, someone knocked on our door during a bad rainstorm with thunder and lightning, the works. The wind had whipped the boat off the mooring, and it took us a bit to get it all OK again. We did have fun, though, those years. Then we rented at Keuka Lake for a few years. The kids would waterski, and they loved it. Chuck drove the boat and usually had to stop for something when someone fell off. But we all had a good time."

They sold the boat to help with college tuition for the girls. "We hadn't really been using it much. We tried snowmobiling next, then downhill skiing. One time Chuck went to Whiteface Mountain in the Adirondacks with some guys to ski. When he returned, he said, 'I have to do one or the other, either downhill ski or golf.' He was afraid of hurting himself in one of the sports, so he gave up skiing and stuck to golf."

As Kathryn, Ellen, and Keith grew up, the girls finished college, Keith became a carpenter, and all started their own careers. Chuck and Joan decided to go south for part of the winter.

"Chuck and I went to Myrtle Beach and Florida. Myrtle Beach was more affordable, and the weather was more suitable for us. At first we had a studio apartment with a Murphy bed, no laundry or phone, and we played golf at Island Green Country Club. We had a good time. Then we rented other places, and in 2000 we found Sandy Shores, which was right across from the ocean. We had a little problem with water leaking through the floor from an upstairs apartment, but the owner came and, after we all mopped up, took care of things. They are all very nice people, retired majors in the Salvation Army."

Since Chuck's death, Joan has continued to vacation in the same place. A couple of years ago though, after shopping at a golf store, she experienced weird feelings and had pains that she thought might indicate a heart attack. She knew she could not drive, called 911, and spent the night in the hospital. Tests showed that she needed a stint. She had a heart attack that night in the hospital and had surgery the next morning. Thank goodness…thank God…she recuperated very well.

"During our marriage, we had three dogs. Chauncey, number one dog, was adopted from Lollypop Farm Humane Society. Chauncey chewed part of a chair, and I repaired it with stitchery. He was hit by a car as he was going to follow Keith during his morning paper route. Britton, number two dog, was always so happy to see Chuck when he came home from work. Overly excited, Britton would pee all over Chuck's leg. You had to be careful. But then came Bruin, a black Lab who was a character. He chewed our new box mattress, and I repaired it with duct tape. Years later, when we got a new mattress, Chuck saw the duct tape for the first time and asked what had happened there. I had never told him. Poor Bruin was killed in the road by another speeder. Chuck said, 'No more dogs.'

"Later Keith wanted a pedigreed German shepherd named Buster. So we had him for a while. We had a fenced-in backyard, but he would jump the fence, run around the house, and sit on our front steps. We closed the kitchen off with the portable dishwasher, but we'd come home and find him sitting in the living room. He'd jump the dish-washer. A couple years later, Keith decided to go to Texas, and Chuck said, 'If you go, take the dog.' He did. Keith works in films now, and it's fun to look for credits with his name printed. The girls each married nice guys, and I have four grandchildren."

Sports were always part of the couple's lives. "Chuck's brother talked him into hunting. He outfitted himself and left, stayed one day, and came home. He couldn't kill a deer.

"Our children suggested we should try bowling. We did and bowled for over twenty years in a couples league. We had a backyard pool, too, and had a lot of good times with it. My dad was the first into the cold water when we opened it every late spring."

Joan's family and Chuck's family all lived within a few miles of each other.

"My husband was a handsome man, and he kept in shape. He was funny and took care of our family well. He maintained and built things. When he was younger, he went to RIT for a semester until the GI bill ran out. He was very happy to be home and just tinker around our home. During bad weather we'd go to the community center to work out. I'd be doing aerobics on one level, and he'd walk the track above. He'd yell down to me, 'Hi, sweetie!' When we walked together, I would walk ahead, circle back to him, and walk with him, then ahead, and back."

Joan was always into cooking and baking, decorating, sewing, and crafting. The two of them made and kept a very welcome home.

And so, Joan, what are your views on marriage, and what would Chuck say?

"Chuck probably would say, 'We had a good marriage.' I would say that some things could have been different, but growing your marriage is to be accepting and acting maturely. Act like a child and you get nowhere; you only get grief. The years went by very quickly. I don't know where the years went. I remember bits and pieces, especially the good times. I think everyone goes through the idea that 'I want to pack my bags' but don't. I think today women are more educated and seem to want to have their own full-time career. When a couple gets married, instead of working out their problems, someone sometimes just says, 'Get out.' It's been made too easy to leave. And maybe one person is too stubborn to contact the other one. I think the only thing I would not tolerate is cheating, which seems to go on quite a lot.

"We always worked things out. We each would get angry at times, but it's a give-and-take in a marriage. You can't put the other person down. I've seen couples who just put down each other constantly. I think I would never put up with that."

Joan and Chuck devoted themselves to each other, to their families and then their children. They participated in local activities and the whole family was on the go. They did what it took and stayed happy.

Charles Van Velson passed away in October, 2007.

Jane and Phil Lehrbach
December 26, 1954

Kisses and compromises did it for us.

A Little Bit of History

On the late 1940s and the 1950s, college campuses were filled with students eager to earn a degree, stay at the four-year institution they enrolled in, do their families proud, make friends, and maybe meet the love of their life. Potsdam, New York, had two colleges across the street from each other: Potsdam State, with about six hundred students, and Clarkson College of Technology (CCT), with maybe a thousand men, no women. Potsdam had two colleges within it: the Crane School of Music and the Elementary Teachers College. CCT offered degrees in a few engineering fields and business management.

Life was pretty straightforward and reflected the United States' climate of postwar growth and peace-seeking people. Potsdam's main education building was on Elm and Main

Streets, and the stately statue of Minerva stood alone in the main foyer. Old Main, CCT's main building, was across the street, and the campus had some newer brick-type structures. Most of the college and community buildings were made of locally quarried reddish sandstone. Sandstone was everywhere.

Dorms were on the top floors of fraternal organizations, in private homes, over stores, and in Quonsets, which were World War II inventions—a kind of college longhouse unit. Greek organizations thrived, and new ones formed occasionally. They were important socially. Frat guys and sorority girls hung together, and once you were the boyfriend or girlfriend, you were somewhat a part of their Greek group, too. To be "pinned" was a ceremony often accompanied by fraternity serenading. A guy would give his girlfriend his fraternity pin, which symbolized being engaged to be engaged.

Fraternities and sororities had their own houses where a certain number of members could live and eat, but all members were welcome to hang out and party. The fraternity members spent time on party planning, decorating, and figuring out food and drink and music, all based around a theme that everyone dressed up for.

Sigma Delta Fraternity, the one Phil was in, was the second fraternity to form in the early 1900s. On St. Patrick's Day in 1904, fourteen juniors and seniors chartered their fraternity, and twenty years later, Sigma Delta bought the Manor House on Prospect Place for a few thousand dollars and remodeled it. It was known for over seventy-five years as the "House on the Hill." The Elbow Room in the basement was known for the parties held there.

The Potsdam sororities started when Potsdam was a "normal school", an experimental at first, program to solely train teachers. Alpha Delta Kappa began as the Alpha Literary Society to give girls a chance to debate. The first evidence of this group was in the 1800s and by 1925, it became a social group. The girls wore purple jackets with white piping. Adorning the breast pocket was a crest with an owl, perhaps representing a quest for wisdom. This sorority, too, purchased a lovely home with a cobblestone front porch at 29 Elm Street. Girls lived there, gathered there, had their meetings there, and had a housemother and hours to abide by.

Note: Unfortunately, Sigma Delta had its charter revoked in 1999. The famous House on the Hill was vacant for a few years, condemned, and then bought by the town in 2006. In 2012, the fraternity made a comeback and is housed on campus, across the river and up the hill. Alpha Delta also had some troubles and has been disbanded for some time.

Girls wore skirts and sweaters or jumpers and turtlenecks, snow pants or a ski suit in the winter, leotards and boots, bunny fur hats, and maybe matching mittens. Boys wore slacks, some corduroy; sweaters and turtlenecks; and maybe a sport jacket with a knit hat. Everyone dressed nicely for occasions; that would be stockings for the girls and a tie for the guys.

It was a dependable world but with narrow choices. Most students followed the creed set before them, and most everyone was content. Students from both colleges trudged across the Raquette River bridge to the unheated wooden arena to watch the Clarkson ice hockey team during the long winter. The stamping of feet on the floors could have been to cheer the team on but more so to keep warm. The winter Ice Carnival, held over several days, was stellar, with exquisite ice statues designed and made by students, skating races, student shows, dances, a parade, king and queen crowning, and of course fraternity parties. Most every student from each campus participated in some way. It definitely was part of the scene in Potsdam. In the 1930s, during the Depression, the carnival was invented to help the community through those tougher times.

It was in this milieu that Jane Paul and Phil Lehrbach went to school, Jane pursuing a teaching degree and Phil, a business degree.

"We met in Potsdam. I was walking down Elm Street with my girlfriends, and Phil and a bunch of Sigma Delta guys were walking behind us. He picked up a snowball—it was a hard one—and threw it and accidentally hit my head. He felt so badly he called me up that night to apologize and asked if I would go the ice hockey game with him. He was dating Jan, one of my roommates at the time, and I had a date with someone else. Well, Roseann ('Scotty') was going to the game with Ted, who was Phil's roommate, and Roseann said, 'Come on, we'll have a good time if we go together.' So, I broke my other date and went with Phil to the game. I didn't kiss him good night that night, but he asked me out to three of the Ice Carnival events. Actually I had a cold sore on my lip, and I didn't want to kiss him. Phil thought I was playing hard to get."

The Alpha girls were close and did everything together. Jane said, "Joan Gurley, Jan Beer, and I—the three Js—sat together in our classes. We were frivolous and had fun meeting people with different experiences. Like Scotty, who wore an earring in one ear; that was very different for us at the time. I never had worn high heels until high school graduation and, of course, wore them as a college girl. There were five of us who lived in the big room of the Alpha Delta house at 29 Elm Street: Marie, Bea, Rosie, Janet, and me; Kay and Peggy lived down the hall. We played bridge all the time, it seemed. We just threw our hands in if someone had no honors, our style. We did study, too, as we all wanted to get our teaching degrees and have a career. It was a wonderful period of our lives."

Phil remembered the fraternity parties at his Sig house and how the guys would all decorate for parties. "For the pirate party, we really wanted to waterproof everything, so we put black plastic all around the rooms, the stairways, and downstairs. I think we sprayed water on each other. We created a different atmosphere."

But then every party at the house had a theme, and everyone got into the swing of it, dressing for it and enjoying the decorations, the food, and the drink.

"We wore plastic trash bags to the pirate party, and everyone had squirt guns," Jane recalled. "We sat on the floor singing and went down to the Elbow Room singing more drinking songs.

It was in that darkened room that Phil kissed me. Kind of nice. And we kept on dating."

Phil was a year ahead of Jane, and when he graduated, after the senior ball, he pinned her. That was an occasion. He went off to Germany as a ROTC soldier for a year.

"Being pinned was nice, but we decided we would also date other people. I dated all year long and went to my senior ball with Jim Hudson. On Valentine's Day my senior year, Phil sent me a huge bouquet of roses with a note that said, 'Watch that snowball.' When he was away, we wrote to each other a lot. When I didn't get a letter, I turned his picture upside down. During one of his college summers, he worked at Kodak in Rochester, saved a little, and bought me a set of pearls in his senior year.

"A bunch of us Potsdam graduates had interviewed for the Rochester City School district, all were hired, and I was assigned to teach at school number forty."

The Rochester City School District in those days was among the top with many successful innovations. It was even studied as an exemplary school model in some teaching colleges. They offered the second highest salary in the state: $3,000 annually.

"Four of us lived together in an apartment, and we all were dating at the same time. Phil's discharge came a little early from the signal corps in Bremerhaven. He came into our apartment in his dress uniform and, boy, did he make a statement. He was a second lieutenant who, while serving in Germany, had skied in the Alps and dated a few German girls, too. But he was back in Rochester with me and started interviewing with different companies. He brought a little MG car home from Germany. When I went home to Harrisville for the summer, Phil kept zooming up to see me in that racy car. He'd rev up that engine, and the little village could hardly handle the commotion."

Harrisville, New York, on the Oswegatchie River, is twenty miles east of Carthage, seventeen miles south of Gouverneur, a few miles from Fort Drum, a tad out of the Adirondack Mountains, and in Lewis County. If you took routes 3, 812, and 9, you'd find it. Last count, there were about 628 people living there. A feature was Scanlon's Bakery on Main Street. The 1940 census lists Jane's dad as Kyler Paul, born in 1898; her mom, Mildred; and siblings Carol and Robert. Jane graduated from high school in the class of 1949 and went directly to Potsdam State. In the 1930s the CCC, Civilian Conservation Corps, was active there, building and sawing down trees. During the war, and only briefly, German prisoners were held there.

"Once when he was visiting me in Harrisville, Phil came into the dining room and lit up a cigarette. My father was appalled. We didn't smoke in the house; we just went out behind the woodshed."

Needless to say Phil didn't make an impression on Kyler, who was president of the school board. None of the local boys would have smoked.

Jane continued, "My father wanted me to marry one of the country boys. Phil had impeccable manners and a clever imagination that the local boys never showed. My parents had met Phil's parents, who lived in West Irondequoit. Phil's mom, Henrietta, was bedridden with arthritis and loved to have me stay there at their home."

Phil's mom had told him that Jane was the nicest girl he had dated. "Phil's family courted me, too," said Jane. "Phil's mom adored him; he was her baby. She had three daughters, and one son who had passed. She had been a teacher and was a Cornell graduate, and we both just loved books.

She was a Quaker from Popular Ridge and was very interested in everyone. She was especially interested in teaching; we had that connection. She really wanted all of us to use her home as a refuge. His dad, Henry, was a civil engineer graduating from Cornell, Phi Beta Kappa.

"The second year I taught, we girls gave up the apartment because none of them except me taught on the west side of the city. I got a room at Lakeview Park on the third floor by myself.

"Phil would come over after work almost every night. He would throw a tiny stone up to my window to let me know he was there. We cruised Lake Avenue in the MG all the way to the lake. That was nice as I was lonely. One night Phil and I were sitting on the steps at the Cross home where I lived, and he gave me a diamond. We were engaged. It was the shortest engagement ever; that was in October, and we were married in December.

"We were married the day after Christmas, December 26, 1954, at three p.m. in the Grace Episcopal Church in Carthage. It was about twenty-five miles from our family home. That church celebrated one hundred fifty years recently. We were Methodist but went to that church for holidays. I wore my sister's beautiful satin dress, and after the cocktail reception, we went on our honeymoon. We have a going-away picture with my girlfriends Joan Gurley, Rosie Grunert, and Ginny Greco, and me. We all dressed similarly, wore little hats.

"We traveled to Vermont for three days to ski. Phil went to the higher slope, and here was Jane…me…on the rope tow with Ginny's ski pants. When we went out, they wouldn't serve me alcoholic beverages because I looked too young, even though I was twenty-three. I didn't bring my license or birth certificate as proof of age. We had fun though. It was our honeymoon."

Jane and Phil returned to Rochester—Jane to the city school district and Phil to Heinrich Seibold. They had a second-floor apartment on Lake Avenue and eventually brought home their first baby, Jeffrey, in February 1956. (Author's note: It was on that second floor that I, as a very green mother-to-be, in April 1956, received lessons from Jane on how to bathe a baby. Jeffrey was the model.)

"In those days, we could not teach past being four or so months pregnant. I asked if I could work until Christmas, and they said yes. But then what would I do? I got a job at GMAC on West Avenue taking care of loans. I took the city bus to and fro. We got rid of the MG and got a car where we could take the baby and all the stuff that goes with carting a baby.

"The night that Jeffrey was born, prior to the birth, Phil and I met some friends, drank Manhattans, and went to a Clarkson versus University of Rochester basketball game. I was nervous before we left. My contractions started at the game, and I was timing them. I had a bag packed in the trunk. Well, we got to Rochester General on West Avenue on time, and Jeffrey was born four hours later. I stayed there for a week. He was colicky. You could hear him coming down the hall crying, and when Phil came, I could hear him, too, coming down the hall with those big rubber boots. Another girl and I went to the scales to weigh ourselves every day at the hospital. They kept new mothers and their babies in the hospital much longer in those days. We moms got a little used to the routines, learning some new baby things, and made friends with others.

"We stayed there on Lake Avenue until September when Phil's mother said, 'How about moving in with us to save money to buy a house?' No one was upstairs at the Franklin Road house in Irondequoit, so she said, 'You could move and have all of the upstairs.' So we moved in. The house was built of used restored bricks from Kodak. I always thought it would be nice to live there and own it later. We lived there for about a year. I was the housekeeper and the caregiver for Grandma."

Phil was making a business call at First Federal Bank and inquired about home owning. The bank official said, "Hey, there's a cute little house on Helen Road. You could get it for a song."

"We scraped it together somehow, and for eighty-three dollars a month with taxes, we were in a nice ranch in a residential area south of the University of Rochester. It was in one of the few free school tax areas, and I think the year's taxes were something like sixty-three dollars," added Jane.

"We worked on the house, and one time we were getting the cellar all fixed up so we could have a party. We laid our own tiles and smeared black tar on the basement floor as prep. Well, people came, and we were doing the twist in the basement…The girls kicked off their shoes, and before we knew it, there was black pasty stuff all over their feet. And all over everywhere. What a mess! But Chuck Schindler and I sure did have fun doing the twist."

Author's note: Black must have been the color. I remember that one sunny summer afternoon I drove down her street with my little son, going to visit her and her son, and what did I see in front of her house? Jane had somehow dragged her living room couch out on the driveway and was finishing up dyeing it, having mixed up several packages of Rit. She dyed her couch black. She is a doer.

Jane returned to teaching, and Jeff joined another toddler (my son Doug) at the babysitter's on school days.

Their second child, Melissa, was born with a congenital hip problem and was in a full-body cast for nine months. Jane stayed home during the day and taught speed-reading at night at the Rochester Business Institute and soon, Jeff started school in the city.

When Phil's parents passed, Phil and his siblings inherited the house. Because it needed a fair amount of work, the house was sold and Phil and Jane went looking for a larger home to accommodate the five of them as Kerstin, their third child had arrived.

Phil had a friend who was a builder and he was starting a new street for future homes. Phil took Jane to see it.

"I thought I was coming to the boonies. Penfield was a small town, and I just knew I was going to be lonely out there. I didn't think I was going to like it. Our friend Ginny had moved to the same town and said, 'It's going to be all right. You can get to Pittsford Plaza in fifteen minutes.' Well, Phil designed it, and when we moved in, it was a sea of mud. There were about four or five homes on the street; the terrible Pamela Moss murder case occurred only a few blocks away, and we were all scared. But now, fifty-two years later, we've stayed in this one house of ours. Our cellar is clean finally, and we are thinking we might move to a smaller place.

"We have had some ups and downs—and some medical issues—but we're here. We've had some trials and tribulations, but we've come through them. It's been wonderful with kisses and compromises."

Phil added jokingly, "As long as it goes Jane's way."

"He has those German roots, and when he wants to, he puts his foot down," Jane said. "When some marriages don't work, I think it must not have been true love in the first place. Phil's sense of humor helps. He has a belief that everything will be OK in the end."

"We'll get through whatever this is," he added.

"Once," Jane remembered, "when Jeff had a tonsillectomy and he hemorrhaged, we had to go to the hospital, and it was bad, Phil said, 'He'll be all right. We'll be all right.' I was a wreck; I'm a worrier and type A.

"I retired after twenty-five years teaching in Penfield and seven more years subbing, thirty-two in all. Phil retired from Merkel Donahue after thirty-five years. With three children, many cats and dogs, we hardly had time to have affairs. We kept busy with our family and marriage.

"Kisses and compromises are the way for us," said Jane, "A sense of humor and each of us doing hard work and a lot of things together."

College sweethearts, Jane and Phil seemed to have done it all. They've had fun, worked hard, golfed, enjoyed music and dancing and stayed fit. They love their family, love doing for others, have a respect for each other. They've had more than their share of medical issues and seem to have kept ahead of them most of the time by supporting one another.

Phillip Lehrbach passed away in May, 2014.

Bev and Stu Silvester
August 13, 1960

Faith kept us together.

"The opportunities we have had through our marriage and through Stu's work are both humbling and fantastic," said Bev. "We have seen people's lives change as they yielded their lives to the Lord as well as watched our own lives take a path we didn't expect. It's all God's work. It seemed like every time we've done something, something else was added to our lives. We worked hard in our church, and once were even given a Hawaiian trip as a gift. We never expected to own a home, but we did, and nice ones, too—just never expected so many perks. It was God's hand of blessing upon us and because of our marriage to each other."

Stu said, "One of those experiences was this. We were sent to Africa, and for seven weeks we worked there." Stu's been to twenty countries, speaking to missionaries and sightseeing.

"We built a church in Zambia to honor the son of friends of ours. The boy had met death by a crocodile. Sad. That family came to our town in Canada every four years, and our church supported them. When I returned to Canada, I traveled to the Maritime Provinces. The people there had the land to have a church but not the means to build it. I re-counted our church building in Africa where many hands helped and thought, 'If we can take a team to build a church in Africa, why can't we build a church right here with volun-teers?' My son-in-law Bruce is a builder, so I asked, 'Would you design a nice little church that we could build in one week? I'll get some people.' At the same time, I was asked to speak about our trip to Africa. At the end of that talk, I asked, 'How many would like to go the Maritimes to build a church in one week?' Twenty-six people volunteered.

"That became the beginning of building twenty-three churches across Canada. We called the project Baptist Builders. Bev helped with the food. A tent was provided, and overall four hundred people across Canada worked: skilled and unskilled people, churchgoers and non- churchgoers. Volunteers said, 'Best week of my life.' God laid it on our hearts to do that. The first was Emmanuel Baptist Church in Digby, Nova Scotia. Another one was Faith Way in Woodstock, Ontario, and Golden in British Columbia. God provided. He gave us the right son-in-law. Someone would provide the lumber; lots of others volunteered to do many things. The trip to Africa started it all. Who knew? People were amazed. The power of people serving God as volunteers."

"And that was after Stu had retired," said Bev. "The Lord provided everything at the right time. Way back, when we were just married, we had to decide whether Stu would go to seminary or if we'd buy a house and settle into life in Sarnia. Stu was working for a synthetic rubber company. We had two little girls and were living in an apartment. Going to seminary meant moving to Toronto and my giving up the road to teacher certification. But we both decided it was the right way for us. Over the years God has given us this and that. He worked it out for us all the time. Opportunities come when we are willing to trust God."

Said Stu, "Bev's dad thought we were nuts making this kind of choice. I went to my pastor, as I knew he would give me good advice, and said, 'You may think I'm foolish, but I really believe I am being called by God into ministry.' My pastor said, 'I've been waiting for you. I really think you should do this. I encourage you. I think it's God's will, Stu.'

"In order to do this, I first had to be accepted. Well, at age twenty-eight, I was accepted at seminary. Then three things had to happen. We had to get an apartment, had to get a babysitter, and Bev had to get a job in Toronto. I left for a day, drove my old T-Bird to Toronto, and in one day all those things happened. We found an apartment within walking distance of the school where Bev was to work, and a wonderful person came as a babysitter.

"We have been blessed beyond our wildest imagination. God has guided us in everything. Once, when our little girl was sick, we had a prescription for a medication but no money to buy it. I was out doing visitations with some seniors. I was leaving a place, and this older lady slipped something in my hand. I told her I would be glad to put the money in the box at church, and she told me she'd had something tell her that I needed some help just then. I looked in my hand and there was a five, a two, and a one-dollar bill in my hand. I went to fill the prescription, and the meds equaled $7.95. We have total trust in God to provide."

"The Lord looked after everything at the right time," said Bev. "Stu's dad phoned one day and said, 'The old farmhouse we used to live in is now for sale again for twenty-five hundred dollars.' Stu's great-grandfather was a builder from England and had come here and built that house in about 1896. It had been sold, and now the current owner wanted to keep the one hundred forty-five acres but sell the vacant farmhouse. None of his brothers were interested. We were living in an apartment but thought that this was an opportunity. We have had chances put in front of us. God puts them there, so many. We were able to purchase the house for eighteen hundred dollars and had it for thirteen years. We worked hard fixing it up, cutting the bushes, making it all nice. It was a great farm experience for the kids. We vacationed there a couple of weeks each year. The taxes were thirteen dollars annually. When the kids became teens, they really wanted to be closer to water for their vacation time, so we sold it for twenty thousand dollars, and with that money we were able to buy a nice place near water. All that was God's work."

"The Lord has always directed my life," Stu continued. "Dr. MacBain, my pastor in Sarnia, came to Toronto to a new church for him, the Forward Baptist Church. I was at seminary in Toronto and had just accepted another summer job with Dr. Pipe in Simcoe and his church, two hours away. By the grace of God, Dr. MacBain was able to arrange for me to stay in Toronto instead, and that was the beginning of my working with him. What an experience. For five years I learned valuable lessons."

"When Stu became pastor at the Bramalea Baptist Church, the church was a few years old. It grew and grew and, before we knew it, we needed to build a bigger building. Stu had seen just the place: six acres at a busy crossways, across from a new mall. It wasn't a given that we could purchase this land, but God directed this, too," said Bev.

"When we received the call that the land was ours," Stu said, "I do know what happened. God answered our prayers."

"The marriage, the working with and for Jesus and God, has blessed us in so many ways. Just the other day," said Bev, "all I wanted was a new refrigerator, and Stu thought it would be nice to have a garage in the south, especially when we leave a car and go to Canada for so many months."

And what do you think showed up? A home with not only a new refrigerator but also a double garage—and four doors away from their current home. The new home became theirs, and their current home was purchased within a couple of weeks. These are not coincidences. They are God's work, and Stu and Bev know when he's showing them what to do.

"I went to school with Allen, Stu's brother, through grade thirteen," said Bev. "His brother took the yearbook home, and it had my picture in it, along with remarks that I went to a club for Christian kids. Allen had told me about the Youth for Christ held on Saturday nights, and so I went. I noticed Allen's brother, who ushered, and thought he was a nice guy, but who would want the name of Silvester? One night after the Youth for Christ meeting, I needed a ride home, and Stu had room in the car. There were four other girls in the car. He dropped me off and said good-bye, and later that same night he called me at my home. But I wasn't home. I had gone out with a girlfriend to bowl. Stu couldn't quite understand that I wasn't home and kind of quizzed my mother. He did call again and asked me to go to a football game. The stadium was close to my home, and we went to the game and watched the Sarney Imperials and a US team. We held hands, and that was the beginning."

"I asked her if she wanted to help with the Youth for Christ. It was a soul-winning class where we reached out to others, and I was involved with the youth. Billy Graham had started the organization, and there we were, about five hundred young people involved. I participated in the Saturday morning radio broadcast and was on the board. I asked her if she wanted to be in a singing quartet and found she wasn't eligible because she wasn't yet eighteen. (Bev added that Stu did not know she could not sing.) I was several years older and was a little embarrassed because she seemed more mature than the other women I dated."

Bev said, "I was going to teachers' college in London, Ontario, and came home on weekends. We wrote letters back and forth, three letters each week. Mail was faster in those days. We dated all fall, and over Christmas he gave me my first present from him.

"Stu had dated a lot, playing the field, but was not limiting it down to one girl," she added. "He asked me to go skating one time, and I said I was booked. I was interested in another guy, too. So Stu asked another gal and went to the same place we did."

"Bev's background was a little different than mine. Her mother went to church but was not strong in her faith. Her dad was not a Christian and had a personal situation. Bev was not particularly happy with her family and a little embarrassed, too. I came from a very strong Christian Baptist background and kind of wrestled with this difference.

"I dated a lot. One gal spoke to her mother in a disrespectful way, so I knew she was not for me. Bev was nice— and pretty, too. Anyway, in February we went to a young people's retreat out of town, and there we got to know each other a little better. And then we became engaged. I had this ring in a box in a bag in my jacket. Bev's brother picked up the jacket, and actually the box fell onto the floor without anyone really knowing what it was. Boy, it almost didn't happen the way it was supposed to."

Bev said, "I was young, and I was not happy at home. I was getting my teaching certificate and planned on teaching. The idea of getting married fell into place a little easier. We decided we would get married in August and I would start teaching in September."

One of Stu's first jobs was as a Fuller Brush salesman, going door to door. "And would you believe it? The first street I was to work on was the street Bev was to live on; she wasn't there then, but in the future. When I met Bev, I was working for Polysar, a synthetic rubber company. It was government owned, and you could get away with almost anything. The guys would tell me I was working too fast and showing them up. My hardworking farm background did not fit into that factory setting. I could never see myself staying there for the rest of my life.

"From the time I was eighteen, I looked into the possibility of being trained for the ministry. Ten years later I was still looking into the possibility. My mom had prayed that one of her five boys would go into the ministry, and she thought I was probably most suited. By then Allen and Roger had both gone to the seminary before me. My mom had been suffering from cancer and died. Her prayers for me had ended. She had gone to heaven. I really admired my mom's faith and her wisdom, and I thought a lot about what she thought of us going into the ministry. When I was going with Bev but also with another gal, my mom said, 'Why are you looking far afield when you have a gal like Bev right here?' The right words at the right time. In the middle of the night I would pray to the Lord, 'What should I do?'"

So plans were made, and Bev and Stu were married August 13, 1960.

"Just before that, Bev's dad said to me, 'If you wait another year, there is a lot next to us, so you could build right next door to me.' I told him thanks but no thanks. I'd rather have his daughter than the lot. We couldn't have afforded a home then but didn't want to live next door to them either," said Stu.

A big wedding was performed at the Baptist church where Stu was active in a number of areas, and the Silvesters started married life in an apartment in Sarnia.

"My first year of teaching was grade five, but I needed two years to get a certificate," Bev said. "Well, the first Christmas, I found I was pregnant, and in those days one couldn't teach in the later stages of pregnancy. I taught until the end of April, and the baby was born in August. I planned on going back in January, still working on my certification, and did get a job that was to start then, but that December I found I was pregnant again. I taught that time through June, and our second child was born in August. Stu's brother Grant's wife took care of the baby; I did some short-term sub teaching and was still lacking months for certification."

"Are you interested in mission work?" posed Stu one day.

During the summer when the children were one and two years old, a few decisions were made that led them to load up a U-Haul and head to Toronto—to the seminary for Stu and back to teaching for Bev.

"The girl who babysat was a godsend; she came by bus and charged very little," Stu recalled.

"And we lived very frugally. We took pop and chocolate out of our life," added Bev.

"I was in first-year seminary and sang bass in the quartet, traveling around on weekends. Bev was home with the kids and her schoolwork. Then, in the first summer after seminary, they wanted us to go out to church to get experience. I was called up to do Home Missions by a pastor who had a church two hours away. The pastor said to me, 'I'll give you lots of experience.' He needed me, and I did get the experience. One day I spoke six times. It was a baptism by fire. I stayed there six days each week and came home on Mondays for a day. Those were two tough months, but we kept going. Bev went to Sarnia and stayed with her parents most of the summer."

"I took extra teaching courses in Sarnia, and Mom babysat. Stu would come home to Sarnia for the one day. Pastor Pipe, the one Stu worked with, said we could stay at their place in Simcoe while they were on vacation a couple of weeks. We did that. We packed up and went for two weeks," said Bev.

"What we didn't realize was that there were a couple of twenty-year-olds living there, too…the pastor's kids. They worked, and I had to have a big meal for them at twelve noon each workday. It was a small fruit-growing community, and migrant workers would just show up at the door for lunch. They knew there was always a welcome and a meal. It was slightly overwhelming for me at age twenty-one as there were so many chores in someone else's home, and with a two- and three-year-old.

"Stu continued his summer work there; we continued to not have much and were just busy and frugal. Stu had one white shirt; it was all he owned and had to wear it on Sundays. One day I was ironing it and I burned it, making holes in the back. Well, he had to wear it. I told him to leave his jacket on. So, after the service, we went to lunch. It was warm so he took his jacket off, and there were the holes. Life's embarrassing moments."

"The second summer I worked with Dr. MacBain turned into five years working with him," said Stu. "I went to school three of those years full time and then a couple more, part time. I learned a great deal from him. He was a great pastor, and just watching how he handled people and pressures helped me. I also experienced going through a church-building program. I became an associate pastor of Christian education and youth. I did get my theologian degree and continued education in my field. We moved from the west end of Toronto to the east end and lived in apartments for nine years. In 1969, I was called to be a pastor at the Bramalea Baptist Church. It had been built in 1964, and I was to be the first full-time pastor. Bramalea was Canada's first suburban city. We ended up staying at that church for twenty years."

Bramalea was a planned community with accommodations for government, theater, communications, and industry, as well as being a residential growth area.

"Our third child was born in 1967. I continued my courses, training to be a librarian, and just that summer, in Bramalea, they were hiring librarians. Another godsend as I was hired," said Bev.

"All Bev's money went to paying down our house. We bought a side-split home in a nice neighborhood of Bramalea. We were always very careful with money.

"I visited every home in the neighborhood, and our church attendance doubled in six months," Stu said. "We had to move to the high school auditorium for Sunday services, and we started to look at building a new church. We ended up selling that building and property and bought five acres in the heart of the city right across from a new mall. The location was a strategic corner at a busy crossroads, very centrally located and visible to all people. We ended up getting that acreage, and there was one acre left. We found out it was owned by the department of highways/planning, and the extra lot was going to cost six thousand dollars and probably not available, as it was all wrapped up in red tape. We were told, 'This may not work.' Someone called me at home and suggested we have a prayer meeting on the acreage. So we did. We prayed, 'Lord, we want this corner.' The next day we had a call from the people we were dealing with, and they said, 'We don't know what happened, but it's all gone through.' I know what happened. God answered our prayer."

"The church we built had eighty thousand square feet, twelve people on the staff, and five choirs. We have wonderful memories of the church in a brand-new community with a lot of young people. Every year our budget went up thousands, and we were giving a lot of money to missions. All three of our girls met their husbands through the young people's group, and all were married there."

Bramalea Baptist Church, BBC as it is called, continues as an outstanding Evangelical church with all kinds of ministries. In 2013, the church held its fiftieth anniversary, and Stu was one of the guest speakers.

"We sold our first home, which was right near the church. The demands of a large church and being so near were taking its toll, stress wise. Someone in the church came to me and suggested that I needed to not be in the mix of things but find another home and work away from it all. We did just that. I drove to work and used Thursdays at home to study."

Bev was a teacher/librarian throughout all of that time. In 1989, Stu resigned from the church and began working for The Fellowship, a group of Evangelical churches across Canada. He traveled across the country, speaking and holding workshops on church growth for our denomination. In 1995, Stu retired from this work.

"But we were still to have another calling. We bought a winter place in the south, and some of the people wanted to have Bible study and a Sunday service. So I was called to that as a pastor and have been doing that for several years. Another blessing."

What are your comments about marriage?

Bev: Stu is very hard working and focused. He didn't take or have time to deal with silly minor things. I held the family together, but Stu was always there as a backup.

Stu: Sometimes I came home for lunch and fixed tomato soup for the kids. We had to be flexible.

Bev: I really believe that way back then, when we made the decision to go to seminary instead of buying a house, God had given all that we needed and more.

Stu: Bev has a lot of wisdom and is incredible with people. I have a lot of respect for her.

Bev: I had a desire to have a good marriage because of what I had seen in my own family. Being the right person is as important as marrying the right person with similar values, dreams, and goals.

Stu: We've had our struggles, problems that could have taken us apart but didn't. Nothing is perfect, and sometimes we bug each other.

Bev: We have three daughters, ten grandchildren, and so far two great-grandchildren who all are blessings to us. We've tried to be models. I think our kids have had more pressures and problems, but they are strong in their faith.

Stu: You work together. Sometimes in my work I was so overloaded…worked about seventy hours a week, so Bev picked up the other responsibilities. She's good socially. We have roles, and the roles cannot be reversed. We have tried to support each other faithfully.

Bev: I would tell people approaching marriage to have similar faith and respect and love each other, following the biblical model and the vows said.

Stu: Some marriages fail because of lack of faith or because one marries a nonbeliever. It's not good to have different value systems.

Bev: Marriages can fail, too, with financial pressures or a degree of selfishness or lack of communication. Respect is very important in a marriage.

Bev: If your marriage isn't strong enough, get help before it's too late.

Stu: Have total trust in God to provide and he will.

Putting every detail of their lives in God's hands, having faith on what's coming tomorrow has been and is the centerpiece for Bev's and Stu' marriage. What a fine example of seeing God's grace on a constant basis.

Maria and Ed Alsfeld
February 18, 1963

I think of him first, and I know he thinks of me first.

Maria's and Ed's parents were finally happy about their marriage when the couple's first child, Eddie, was born a year or so after the wedding He was the first grandson after several granddaughters. Everyone was happy to welcome a boy.

When Maria and Ed had married, she was seventeen years old and he was eighteen. None of the parents were too happy about it at the time. Maria said, "The first time I met Ed, I was fourteen and he was fifteen years old, and we were at Scholl's roller skating rink. He was very cool with his hair slicked back, and he wore a silver shirt. I guess it was love at first sight. We went out from then on. At the time, my cousin MaryAnn was kind of sweet on him, and I told her to get lost. We went together through junior high and senior high, left school, and in the middle of the week, on the eighteenth of February, were married. Our families thought we were just too young."

1963

In February 1963, the first Boeing 727 jet took to the air, the Beatles recorded their first album, and Julia Child's TV show premiered. Willie Mays, of the Giants, and Mickey Mantle, of the Yankees, signed the first of their kind: $100,000 annual contracts. And in Warwick, Rhode Island, two teenagers wed.

"We found an apartment in an old house on the third floor overlooking the beach. Ed's sister came, and we painted the whole thing. After Eddie was born, we moved a couple of times; for a while we lived with Ed's parents and then moved to another rental home."

"We lived in Warwick, and I raced stock cars a few miles away at the *Action* Track of the East in Seekonk, Massachusetts. I drove other people's cars, and we had a lot of racing friends," said Ed.

"Our second child, Wendy, was born, and we had very little room in our place. But we had a lot of friends and had a lot of parties there. I was an only child, and Ed had two brothers and a sister. We lived near family; I was a stay-at-home mom. Eventually we moved next door to my mom."

Maria and Ed also made a decision to take care of foster, or state, children.

The Rhode Island Foster Care and Adoption center says online, "Although this journey is not for everyone, it can be the most rewarding decision you will ever make. The journey can be long and at times frustrating, but we are here to give you support and encouragement along the way for as long as you need or want it."

The journey *was* for them, and they ended up caring for twelve children over the years. The care was to be short term, temporary, frequently as an emergency, and often only for a weekend. Sometimes a child stayed a little longer.

There was one such youngster.

Maria said, "John was ten months old, a year younger than our Wendy. He came for a week. Then a month. Then longer. His mom never came to visit him, and I think John assumed he was staying with us. At this time I was pregnant with our third child. One day he had been playing in the sandbox by the back door when he came in choking. I swept his mouth, checked him over, and called 911. The rescue squad came, and somehow he had found charcoal fluid and drank some. He was in the hospital for three weeks and on the danger list for a good part of that time. His mom never came. We decided to ask the social worker if we could adopt him. When we went to see the judge, I covered myself up with a big coat hiding my pregnancy, as I wondered if maybe the judge wouldn't let us adopt. Anyway, it took a while to finalize the adoption, and in the meantime Billy was born. Then Michael was born. A few years later, John had a paper route and the kids and I would all deliver the newspapers after school. I would push a baby carriage with the newspapers and baby Michael in it."

Maria and Ed had five children and moved once again to Maria's mom's home. The children went to St. Benedict parochial elementary school and then on to the high school. St. Benedict's parochial school turned 100 years old in 2014.

"The kids all had jobs early. One time, when John was a teenager, he came to me and said, 'I want to take Jenny to the movies,' and he asked for money. I told him I had none. 'Dad and I haven't been to a movie in years.' John got a job working for a cleaning office company Friday night and Saturday, and then he could afford to take someone out. Billy worked there for a while, too.

"When John was 18 years old and Jenny, his girlfriend was 16, he told me, 'Guess what Jenny got for my birthday. We're going to a hotel.' I said, "no, you're not going there. If you go to a hotel, I'm calling her father.' They didn't go. About 20 years ago, John married a nice Italian girl but they broke up after a few years. A few months ago he re-met Jenny on the internet and now they're engaged," said Maria.

"Ed's job was seven days a week. He worked most of his life and missed out on some family stuff," said Maria. "I worked at R & R auto supply store, a small family-owned company with a warehouse and five stores," said Ed. "I worked there for forty years, and then it went out of business when the bigger chain stores like Pep Boys and so on came into their own."

To work forty years for one company was more typical of our parents' generation, so Ed working for forty years in one place was quite honorable. The company and he must have liked each other. Auto supply stores have been around for more than a century, ever since the bicycle was a serious mode of transportation.

In 1982, Maria and Ed made a big change. Their eldest had joined the navy, Wendy and John were in high school, and Billy and Michael were in middle school. They decided to purchase a house with three acres of land in nearby Foster. The children in high school did not want to move at all. But, soon after entering their new school, they were quite happy after all.

Foster is just east of the Connecticut border and south of the Massachusetts border and has about five thousand people. There are about a hundred farms in that area. When the Alsfelds moved there, little did they know how extensive their farming career would become!

Ed and Maria raised seven kinds of animals, not counting their pet dogs. They had cows, horses, chickens, turkeys, sheep, pigs, and goats. I find this amazing, as they were not born into farming and had no major initial plan or outline. They each contributed to the construction, the investigations, the raising, and the distribution. They also had various fruit trees and a vegetable garden. This was part of the foundation of their good marriage.

A Little Bit of Information

The animals which were raised by Maria and Ed all had some of the same basic requirements such as good and appropriate housing, proper food, strong fencing and a perch or a run, depending on the animal's specific needs. Some needed safety from predators; the pigs needed be able to wallow in mud; some needed more roaming and grazing land, and some were described as social, therefore requiring more than one in their group. Each group of animals could face specific health issues and therefore needed proper overseeing. Online there are many sites full of information on 'how-to' and there are organizations such as the New Forest Pony Society of North America, American Dairy Goat Organization, National Cattlemen's Beef Association and more for every animal. You can find descriptions of how to select an animal initially, what kind of feed to get, what weight to strive for if marketing, relative statistics and all kinds of pictures of animals. I especially enjoyed seeing Olive, Clove and Pearl, three pretty goats on one of the sites.

"We bought a cow and named it Moo number one. Then we bought another cow and named it Moo number two. Moo number two would break loose sometimes. We bought neutered calves, bottled them, and raised them all for meat. We didn't name them and didn't get too close to them as pets. We had a good-sized pen and some pastures and barned them. We had them for about three years, but they became tough to handle. We'd have to chase them. It was pretty normal to have to do that. The police would hear things like 'Go get Joe's cows,'" said Maria.

"We stopped raising cows after about three years. Cows are pretty dumb," Ed said. "We then got into chickens. We always had chickens from then on. We had twenty-four hens and built a chicken coop. We first had them for eggs. They laid eggs and they could browse, and at night they went in to roost. Chickens are very efficient. I sold some eggs at work."

Maria said, "I ordered some poults (baby hens). I ordered a dozen. Ed came home with about fifty. Ed said, 'They were only a few dollars.' I told him, 'That's not the point, dear.' We had to keep them all under heat until they feathered. We had a lot of eggs."

The turkeys were next.

"We bought some turkey poults when they feathered and kept them until they were big. Ed's grandparents had a turkey farm, and one of them weighed thirty-nine pounds. We raised them for a long time and had lots of food in the freezer."

Ed did all the building of animal shelters, the fencing, and range areas. "Our turkeys had a coop with a branch in it to roost on. Be happy, I thought. There was water on one side and food on the other. They wouldn't cross the branch to eat or drink."

"Besides the animals, we had grapevines, cherry trees, peach trees, five gorgeous apple trees, and beautiful plum trees," said Maria. "I canned everything."

"And," said Ed, "you could eat a peach right off the branch. We planted all of the trees."

"Wendy and Billy had started horseback riding before we made the move to Foster," said Maria, "We had one horse named Added Expense, nicknamed Addy. She was a quarter horse, a bay, a little cranky but very well trained in dressage and hunting. They showed the horse on weekends. We encouraged the children to try everything. Wendy and Bill boarded the horse, and they worked for the woman who owned the stables—cleaning stalls, riding other people's horses, both stable and racing horses—and then their horse could be boarded for free.

Ed said, "A thoroughbred came as a gift from the kids' grandparents, so we had two horses. Wendy grew up, got married, and left Maria and me with the horses. So we knew a little about horses."

Then they got into raising ponies.

"A friend was breeding ponies, New Forest ponies. Over the years, I had a ton of these ponies," Maria said. "I went to Canada and bought two mares from a lady there," Maria continued. "I brought them back; each was pregnant, and each had a foal, which we then sold.

"We had a chestnut mare, Shimmery, whom I trained and had a friend who would show the horse. We had horses for eighteen years, from 1982 to 2000. Jason, one of our horses, was sold to a 4-H'er, and Addy retired from showing. Cheyenne the third horse we had, was Ed's horse. Ed would ride Cheyenne and I would ride Addy through the woods and visit with friends. Sometimes I would get the saddlebags, put some refreshments in them, ride a couple of miles to an area by the quarry in the woods, and meet our friends.

"Well, we had a lot of horses," said Maria.

The Alsfelds raised sheep for a short time.

"We got the sheep so we could spin our own wool from their fleece," Maria explains. "I learned how to knit and was going to do it all. But I couldn't knit too well, and Ed didn't like to eat lamb. It was a short-lived experience."

They then got into goats, which were Maria's favorites. "We raised and registered them with the American Dairy Goat Association. We had a big herd of fifteen to twenty goats and named each after a car track, like NASCAR Nanny and so on."

"We built a nice goat barn, a paddock, opened the gate, and there was a fenced way they could go to pasture," Ed recalled. "Billy and David built a little barn for the goats with a little window in it. There were a lot of goat farmers then. It's a dying breed now."

Maria related, "We brought the goats to a Washington County fair to show. We worked with the 4-H kids and put on cheese demonstrations. We had a lot of fun with them. The goats were awesome, better than dogs. We made goat milk fudge in our kitchen with a bunch of kids. I was active in the Rhode Island Dairy Goat Association and was president for a while. There were about thirty adults in it. They were all very nice people. My own children would say that their mom had gone to a ladies club meeting, rather than say I went to the Goat Association meeting.

"I used to see a lot of goat milk. A lot of dog people would come and get some to raise their puppies on it. One lady was raising Newfoundland's, and to stock up enough, she'd buy some of our frozen goat milk. You couldn't sell it for human consumption without a license but could sell it to people with dogs. We loved to drink it and eat our goat cheese." Goat's milk is easier to digest than cow's milk for those who have difficulties with cow's milk. Swiss chocolate is made from goat milk because the makers think it is the sweetest tasting. Raw goat milk though cannot be sold in Rhode Island retail, only by doctor's prescription.

The next animals to be raised, were pigs. Ed recalled, "A friend, Steve, raised pigs and said to me, 'Why don't you raise pigs?' I built a pigpen quite a few yards away from the house and bought two pigs the first year. We started them on the goat's milk. We bought three more from Steve and then bought a few more. I built a bigger, better pigpen, a beautiful concrete pen, and there was a pool in there for the pigs to cool off. We would get them to market weight in sixteen weeks, about two hundred pounds."

There was a time when Ed's business was closing, and it seemed right for Ed and Maria to buy thirty acres of land. Maria remembered, "I said why don't we build a house on some of the property that we own? I bought some house plans; we revised them and planned to build it ourselves. The house we lived in at the time was a small Cape, and our new house was to be about three times the size. It was a big Cape, a gigantic home to have all the family there. Our son was a contractor and had a lot of builder-type people he knew who could build it."

"We sold the little house on the hill the first day it was listed," said Ed, "and then had no house and no mortgage. We didn't have to worry about money for the first time."

Maria said, "We bought a trailer and lived in it on our new property because the new house wasn't ready. It was a forty-footer or so. I was doing babysitting every day at that time, too. I had five grandchildren—Sarah, Mattie, Sydney, Jonathan, and Erin—to watch. We did fun stuff. Ed's job was about five minutes away, and the grandkids' parents drove about forty minutes to us every day. The farm was the best move for the kids."

" I had the chance to buy a sixty-eight black Camaro with white stripes where I worked; I loved working on it and fixing it all up. When we got into the large acreage property, we needed a backhoe to work some of the land. So I sold that car, and then the fun started. Our son Bill bought a contingent fifteen-acre piece of land, and he, too, was going to build a house. The backhoe was needed to help clear the land."

"Bill, his wife, and two toddlers moved in with us until their house was built," said Maria, "and then John sold his house, and he and his family moved in with us, too. Our new house at Christmas had three young ones, but our big house was ready to welcome everyone. So Bill built his house, and then we gave Eddie five acres between Billy and us, and they moved in with us, too, until their home was built."

Maria started working at the Phoenix House, a recovery rehab center for people with addictions. She had gone to school to get her Certified Nursing Assistant license, Every week at the Phoenix House, by law, the kitchen had to be cleaned totally, with no food left in it. Each Friday she'd fill up the back of the station wagon with any leftover Entenmann's pastries. "Ed would feed the pastry and goat milk to the pigs. The pastry and goat milk made for really good meat. You could cut it with a fork, and we could sell every bit of the meat. Some people wanted to chip in and have us get more pigs. But getting rid of them was tough and became tougher. Ed started getting attached to them. Pigs would be playing with Ed; they'd grab his pants leg. But then they got heavy. When they're about one hundred fifty pounds, they can be a little rough. Ed would scrub the pigpen and scrub the pigs."

They had almost stopped raising them earlier, because of the attachment formed between man and pig. Eventually, raising pigs did end.

"We started going to Florida to visit and dog-sit for Ed's brother. We loved it and started to look around," said Maria.

Ed added, "We bought a home in the South and went back and forth to Rhode Island. The big home up north was wonderful but hard to sell, as taxes were high."

"And the work was getting harder and harder," Maria noted "We'd be healthier in the South. So we put our Rhode Island house on the market, eventually sold it, and now stay in the South with our Corgi dogs."

So why do you think you stayed married for all this time?

Ed: I think we stayed together because we like one another.

Maria: Yes, I kind of like you, too.

Ed: I had a seven-day workweek, and she had the animals. We worked as a team. We built fences, barns, cleared land for the animals, and planned it all. The other part of it is she took care of the kids and me, a full-time job. I never realized how close we were until I got sick a few years ago, and she took really good care of me. It's called *true love.* I was a very sick puppy. I wanted to go, and if it weren't for her, I wouldn't be sitting here now.

Maria: When we go to do something, or make a decision, I think of him first, and I know he thinks of me first.

Ed: Kind of like what we did for the kids. It seems that everything through our whole marriage was for the kids."

She also had an interest in my racing; she supported them and me.

Maria: I don't think you can be a selfish person and have a good marriage. And I think there is no or very little commitment by many people who can't stay married.

Ed: We've had fifty-one years of marriage this year.

Maria: Amazing. We were fourteen and fifteen years old and stayed together all this time.

Each venture into raising animals was a risk Maria and Ed took together, and it sounds like it was worth it. Their marriage became and stayed strong through the work in front of them. I don't know much about raising farm animals, but I do know that in the animal world, there can be ups and downs of illnesses and injuries as well as joy and pride. They weathered it all together.

Elaine and Ray Downs
June 22, 1950

We made the right choice the first time.

They knew each other in junior high school in Bangor, Maine, their hometown. "We were in the same grade," said Elaine, "but lived in different areas of town. We were never close, just knew each other. We were both in Christian Endeavor, which met Sunday nights, so we saw each other then. That was nice, but there was nothing between us."

"I was chasing a girlfriend; she was one of the two girls I can think of whom I might have been interested in. I dated quite a few," said Ray. "Elaine was the third girl I was interested in, and that became so more and more—something about that third girl, Elaine. She was the last girl I ever dated."

"During high school, we didn't date until our senior year," Elaine recalled. "Then there came the big basketball playoffs in Boston. Bangor High had won the state championship and was competing for the New England championship. It was only the second time I had ever been out of Maine. A lot of us went to the big game. My sister, Jeannie, had made reservations at a hotel for two of my friends and me, and she was at another hotel. Ray was there with his friends, too. Well, Bangor didn't win, but we had plans to stay for a certain amount of days."

Ray continued the story: "We had tickets for more days, and with our high school not playing any more, we looked for something to do. One of my friends was going steady with one of Elaine's friends, and he said, 'I'm going to call Peggy.' I told him to ask whom she was here with. He did and said she was here with her friends Gladys and Elaine. So I said, 'Let me have the phone when you're done.'"

"He asked me if I'd go out with him that night. We did and went tramping around Boston Commons and then went to a nightclub," said Elaine.

"At the nightclub we were sort of kicked out because our server said to us, 'You may want to take these ladies out before the show starts.' There was a cover charge and not sure about the show, so we went back to Boston Commons and walked around."

"Two of my boyfriends were Ray's good friends," said Elaine.

"And, the rule of the day was don't date your buddy's girlfriends, but she wasn't going steady with either then."

Ray was always into music and in high school had a band that played at the Bangor Y. Elaine went, and they managed to dance together even though he was performing.

A Little Bit of History

This all occurred in the late 1940s in Maine. Maine is our almost most northern state, certainly one of the largest in the area, and one with a reputation for beauty, independence, and permanence. Tourists visit to experience the serene forests, the ocean around Bar Harbor, and maybe touch into New Brunswick, the Canadian province just up the road. It's gone the route of farming, hunting, textiles, lumbering, and ocean commerce. Samuel de Champlain, the famous explorer, passed through this area and began a fur trade with the Indians. Bangor was settled by families—families with a lot of children—who came north from Massachusetts during the eighteenth century. Maine was part of Massachusetts until it became a state in 1820.

Both the Revolutionary War and the War of 1812 reached well into Maine, into Bangor, and World War II had an effect, too. The state housed a small POW camp for captured German soldiers, and two German spies landed by U-boat on the shores nearby, found their way to Bangor and then by rail to NYC, and later were captured by the FBI. Bangor has been known as the "Lumber Capital" and the "Queen City." The Penobscot River runs through it, and there is much water around, including lakes, bays, and the Kenduskeag Stream. It is northeast of the capital, Augusta. Bangor High School was founded for boys only in 1835, and a few years later, a separate school for girls formed. They joined to become a coed school in 1864. This is the school Elaine and Ray went to, and it still exists today.

The Williston Congregational Church in Portland started the Christian Endeavor in 1881; other cities followed suit. The group's sole purpose was to inspire youth to stay with the church and promote a Christian life. It is now a worldwide organization.

"We decided not to go steady when Elaine went to Westbrook Junior College in Westbrook, Maine. I went to the University of Maine in Orono and was running a dance band three nights a week, playing for private parties, school dances, fraternity parties, and Dow Field Air Base in Bangor. I went to college to try to get an engineering degree. Elaine was at Westbrook having a good time and came home sometimes for the weekends. We'd date then and once in a while go to a fraternity party," said Ray.

"My senior year at Westbrook came, and we were having a senior party there. Ray couldn't come, so I had a blind date that a friend fixed up for me," said Elaine.

"I had a six-piece band, and it had been doing pretty well. We were in the Battle of the Bands, and it was on the same date as Elaine's party. We were against an eight-piece band that even charged less to play. The winning band would get a summer job. Well, we won and had the summer job. The next day I drove over with the Browns, Elaine's folks, to get her now that school was done. I rode back with Elaine and her parents, and the reception was quite cool."

"I went to work for a doctor in Bangor. The fellow I dated had a blue Oldsmobile convertible. Lovely. I still dated Ray, who was then a junior in college, and he bought his first car, a 1930 Buick, which leaked from the ceiling and had no brakes. About Christmastime, Ray proposed."

"And," added Ray, "she took the ring. We had a plan to marry after my graduation."

"Peggy, a good friend, and Curly married and lived nearby. We spent time with them, and we were all having a lot of fun. Well, they had a baby, and when the baby was a month old, Curly had Ray hold it."

"I had never held a baby that young," said Ray.

It kind of encouraged them to move up their wedding date. Elaine Brown and Ray Downs married on June 22, 1950, in Portsmouth, New Hampshire, by the minister who had run the Sunday evening church meeting in Bangor years earlier.

The band was doing quite well, and Ray had enough money to finish college. They lived on campus in a GI trailer. Although not a GI, one could still apply for that kind of campus living. GIs had preferences over non-GIs in those days soon, after World War II.

"Approval came through, luckily," said Ray. "It seemed like where there was a will, there was a way. Elaine drove back and forth to work from there. She worked in Bangor, which was thirteen miles south of campus. That's how we got started."

"One wintry day," Elaine remembered, "Ray insisted in cutting class and driving me to work because it was very icy. He drove, was driving very slowly and carefully, when our car rolled over and landed on its top."

"The first thing she said was 'Darling, keep your feet off the ceiling.' We got out and got help righting the car and a ride to Bangor for a tow truck." Some experience.

"Nineteen fifty-one was a beautiful year for mechanical engineers," Ray said. "I had seven different offers. It was unbelievable. Kodak was right in the middle salary wise. I had been out of the state only once, and that was to Boston in my high school days. I was a country boy. Probably the best job I ever was offered was in Camden, New Jersey. But I flew to Rochester, and just flying over it, seeing the lakes to the south and Lake Ontario to the north, I was impressed. I walked around the city and thought it was clean; it impressed me. I took one of two offers from Kodak and figured if one didn't work out, I'd take the other. Well, I did change to the other job at Kodak and grew to like it. I stayed there thirty-two years more and retired at the age of fifty-seven. Seems like my son Jeff wanted to beat me in early retirement as he recently retired at age fifty-three."

Going to Rochester, New York, they found a home being built by Caldwell and Cook on Sierra Drive in the large suburb of Greece.

"Our first house and our second and third homes were all brand new, so we had input into them all, three new homes. The house on Sierra Drive, our first, was picked from one of four different models, and we made a few minor changes like adding a laundry chute and an extended dormer. At the time, we backed up to a cornfield, but Skycrest, a new road behind us, was eventually built up with homes about 1955. We raised our four children there."

Ray retired in the spring of 1986. "We had been looking for years to decide where to retire and live. We used to meet the Maine crowd in New Hampshire, which was about halfway between them and us, so we knew the area." The Maine crowd was five other couples who graduated from the University of Maine with Ray. "There were eighteen children all together, and they would fall into play as if they had seen each other last week. We went to each other's weddings, kids' parties, kept in touch. So we wanted to keep that going. Actually, now one spouse of each couple has passed on.

"Well, back then, I had decided that we needed to be within four hundred miles of Rochester, because at the time both Jeff and Sharon were married and had bought homes. We could drive the four hundred miles. That put us halfway into New Hampshire. The northern limit of that area for us was to be Lincoln, New Hampshire. We talked with the real estate agent and told him that it was to be a permanent home. Lincoln was a 'tourist' home, a ski area, and most people go someplace else much of the time. He suggested Campton with colleges nearby and showed us an area where they were selling five or six lots with acreage. We bought about three and a half acres with a pond that had peepers. I had played with designing homes off and on. Elaine kind of knew what she wanted."

"I wanted a nice-sized dining room so you didn't have to reset a table or take down anything," Elaine said. "We ended up with a large kitchen and family room and a nice large living room. There were two levels. We had the laundry room downstairs on the same level with the three bedrooms and a bath petitioned off with a living area ready."

"I had already built a wall between the future living room and my shop, which wasn't finished yet, in the basement," said Ray. "Planning the Cider Mill Drive home, we owned two houses for a while. I walked into our bank and said I needed to borrow umpteen dollars for a transition, and the banker said, 'Sure, how much do you need?' and he wrote a check! That was in the mid-eighties."

The Cider Mill home had many windows upstairs and on the lower level, because the views in every direction were wonderful. This was in the White Mountains with only two neighbors nearby, so there were no interruptions in the views as far as you could see. The sunsets were beautiful. The access road out to the highways was finished somewhat, but mainly dirt and stone. You knew you were in the country and in the woods of New Hampshire. Deer, lots of wild turkeys, and moose visited now and then.

"Everyone came and enjoyed our home," said Elaine. "Ray mowed paths for the grandchildren to play on. He tried to maintain the pond in the winter. One time the snow blower broke while he was trying to clean the pond. Mitch, our neighbor, came down and hauled it out of the pond with his backhoe. Sharon, Abbie, Cris, and Sarah all loved to skate there. Sarah would have her little 'store' there and sell hot cocoa. Cris would bring his trucks in the nice weather."

Ray said, "By 1999, it had become too much to take care. It took two or three hours to do snow removal. We hired Cris to help with the lawns, but he had school and sports. Cris knew how to winterize a lawnmower and 'summerize' the snow blower but didn't always have the time. The work was beyond my capacity. Our present home, a patio home in the township of Holderness, is not far from Sharon and Rick so is perfect for us. Our porch faces fields and woods, and we see the birds and a few deer."

"Now we are toying with the idea of using part of Sharon and Rick's land and adding on a new addition for us. It might be a separate home with a little kitchen for a miniature refrigerator, miniature sink, and miniature stove," said Elaine.

"We'll work on it," said Ray. "We'll need room for two desks, one for the computer and the other for my big roll top desk. It'll be twenty-three feet by twenty-four feet or so."

"When we first met, Ray was a Baptist, then changed to Congregationalist—chasing a girl actually—and then later to Methodist."

Ray said, "When we moved to Greece, the first minister who visited us was from Aldersgate United Methodist Church, so that's the church we stuck with. I had headed up the finance committee, and when I was through with that, I was on buildings and grounds. When I was on finance, I used to shoot the ideas down from buildings and grounds. They wanted me to be on both. I said I was going to quit. Well, I just stopped showing up for either committee meeting. Sometimes someone would call at five fifteen on the evening the committee was to meet to remind me to come. But I didn't. That was the only way I could get out of it. I was on the administrative committee when someone said, 'Let's move to ask God to repair our roof,' and I said, 'Christ has more to do than to repair our roof.' Their motion didn't pass. I was on the music committee at first, actually on it before I joined the church."

Music has and is very important in Ray's life. In high school and college, he had a band and frequent gigs. He has written multiple arrangements and led many musicians in a variety of bands that performed several decades ago for dances, more recently for concerts, and presently for pleasure at his own home. It has been a lifelong devotion and love.

"When we first moved to New Hampshire, it seemed that most of the local bands played only John Phillip Sousa. While I appreciated it, I wanted a dance band. I started to get other members to join me in playing big band music, and soon I put together a nineteen- to twenty-piece big band. For a long time I directed and didn't play. Then I retired from directing and just played. Then I got to the point where I was tired of it. The band went on for another five years or so with the name of White Mountain Big Dance Band. When I had played, we'd be gone for the whole night. Eventually that stopped, too.

"I started up a jam session at our home, and different players came, including someone who could hardly play improvisation music. Ellen, a local veterinarian who plays sax; Gabe, an attorney who plays trumpet; and I get together almost every week. Elaine will frequently go to Sharon's and visit on those Tuesday nights. I have a keyboard and a baby grand piano. All four kids had piano lessons, plus Jeff played trumpet, Sharon played the bass violin, Susie played saxophone, and Debbie sang in choirs. I have a library with many arrangements. I had fallen heir to compositions from some Rochester musicians, people who were kind of sick of playing them. They were very good tunes and very good arrangements and ended up in our basement. They moved with us. I wrote some arrangements, too, and they're all here."

Family life was number one with the Elaine and Ray. Besides being content with their homes, they did vacation, too. "We started tenting in 1960, and by 1964, I said, 'I don't want to do this anymore. I don't want to leave at five p.m. after work, pack up, head for the Adirondacks, and not know where our tent is going to be set up," said Elaine.

"So," said Ray, "in 1965, we bought the camp for a thousand dollars. It was near a railway track that was not in use anymore. Each lot was one hundred feet square. There were ties lying around but no railway track. It had been discontinued in the 1920s and torn up in the thirties. The camp was only one floor with no electricity but right on Brown's Tract Pond in the mountains. The next-door neighbor came and helped me—both of us lying on the ground on our backs—try to figure out how the plumbing worked. There was usually something to be done, and then in the mid-seventies, we decided to put on a second floor. We took the old roofing off. Elaine and Sharon pulled nails to save and reuse wood. Sharon's future husband, Doug, helped a lot, too, in producing the current camp. I brought my saw up and cut sizes as we needed them. Some cupboards I made in my basement in Greece, disassembled them, carted them to camp, put them together, and installed them. We put a little deck out back with bench seating. It was lovely, and when you sat out there, you were truly into the trees. We built it the last year Elaine's mother, Mrs. Brown, was here. She thoroughly enjoyed how we had enlarged it."

This is the forty-ninth year at the camp, and with the upstairs bunks, there have been as many as fourteen people, and many times five dogs. Sharon and Rick bought the camp a few years ago, and that very year the state of New York decided some of the camp had to be moved off of state property, about eighteen inches maybe. So the pretty little deck and some of the camp were chopped off, and a new configuration made. The new deck is much larger, in a different direction, and very useful. There is still no electricity, so everyone enjoys the oil lamps and a non-electronic existence.

"I have to keep reminding myself," says Elaine, "that this isn't our camp anymore."

Everyone who takes a boat out or swims without an adult first has to pass Ray's "test," and that is to swim across the lake or to the beach. Fortunately, it is of pond status, which forbids motorized boating, and is very safe.

"Years ago," said Elaine, "the kids would go swimming at night at camp. We made sure they had buddies. They'd jump off the dock and swim in the dark usually down to the beach. But Ray and I would get in the canoe and go up the lake to the other end and watch from the shadows. Then we'd hurry back before they returned so they didn't know we were watching!

"Ray always felt a vacation wasn't a vacation unless we left home. So we went to camp and always went to Maine for a week because that's where both of our families were. I had two siblings, Imogene and Emery. Imogene, called Jeannie, and husband Coly moved to Greece, too, so for their working years, they were close by. But they moved back to Maine when they retired. Ray's sister Barbara and her husband, Jack, were there. He had a brother who was in the Korean War. He came home, went to business school, and a few weeks later died in a car accident. He was four years younger than Ray. One year, 1966, I think, we took all four weeks of our vacation and took the children out west, and we managed to get to the West Coast. Ray planned it, and that's what he enjoys doing.

"Another thing we did," Elaine continued, "was any place we went with the kids, if we were near a presidential museum, workplace, home, library, and so forth, we took them there. Ray and I have been to forty-nine of the fifty states. When he retired, we started on more trips, often with our friends Ted and Priscilla. We went to Vancouver, Texas, Arizona, many places, and even rented a houseboat on Lake Powell with three other couples for six days. We did a lot of sightseeing and always met for dinner someplace.

"On one of our trips home to Maine, when we were living in New Hampshire, we went to Belfast, Maine, where Ray had gone in his childhood. We stayed at the Colonial Gables. I was out walking Sharon's new dog, and two girls who were staying there struck up a conversation. They had been there overnight and were returning home the next day. Well, we figured out that one of the girls was Curly's baby, the one Ray had held many, many years earlier."

"When I got up the next morning, Elaine said, 'There's someone I want you to meet,' and I met the baby I had held."

"Ray and I had the same interests," she said. "We liked outside sports, activities; we liked to ski, did a lot of scouting, and Ray had one or two band jobs a month and rehearsed every other week. Kodak sent us to MIT for a year to 'retread an old engineer.' He had his master's from U of Rochester when Debbie was born. Our goals were the same. As the kids were growing up, we enjoyed their activities. All our vacations were done with the kids. I did a lot of chauffeuring, and I was scout leader for Suzie's troop. I took them to Washington, DC, their last year of scouting, and Ray took them on a canoe trip on the eleventh of June one year, and the black flies were thicker than ever. I instructed the girls how to actually spread the black fly ointment all over every inch of bare skin. Of course they wore short shorts not long pants."

Ray recalled, "My brother-in-law Coly went with me. We were in one tent and the girls in another. I woke up during the night, and the sky was so beautiful I was tempted to wake them up to view it. I didn't, though. Buggy trip."

Scouting was a big part of Ray's life. Troop 321 out of Lakeshore became filled, so Troop 320 was added. "The boys and their dads had to attend the organizational meeting, so Jeff and I went," he said. "They realized I owned a tent and had gone camping so that kind of made me camping chairman. Being a brand-new troop, there wasn't much equipment. Later I became scoutmaster and was active for ten years. When Bill Smith left to form other troops, he invited me to run the Court of Honor and the Eagle Board of Review. One time I went to help Bill put a scout through a lot of questions. Well, it seemed like the shill who was trying to make Eagle just wasn't ready. So I spoke to Bill privately and said, 'What's going on with this kid? He's in no way ready to be an Eagle.' Bill then said he'd had to think of a way to get me there to award me a ten-year plaque. So that was nice, but I was still upset with him.

"I used to run high-adventure trips after I was scoutmaster, usually because newer scoutmasters couldn't canoe or swim. I saved my vacation for it and set the requirements for canoeing, swimming, and lifesaving badges before they could go. One mother called me and wanted to argue the point that her son was a good swimmer and canoeist but had earned no badges. So, I said to her, normally I was in the last canoe and the kids in the front were usually about a half an hour ahead of me. In an emergency, I expected the kids in the front canoe could take care of themselves. Now, can your son do that? Well, that year he couldn't, didn't go, but the following year he did.

"There are scout stories like about Rich Orlando. He could only 'swim' when he touched the bottom. Doug was junior assistant scoutmaster, and I asked him if he could take Rich to his pool at his house and teach him how to swim. I wanted to say that Rich could go on the trip. The lifesaving merit badge is much more strenuous than the swimming merit. Doug did succeed in teaching him, and he went. Rich stayed long enough to get his Eagle, too. He turned out to be a responsible scout and came to call on us after college. He said to me, 'You would never call off a winter campout.'"

Elaine and Ray's four children are all adults with children of their own now. Debbie and Suzie have their doctorates and live in and near Boston with their husbands, Charlie and Dave respectively, and children. Jeff has been a stellar success with his website MyGrocer.com, and Sharon, an art teacher and successful potter, and Rick live nearby in Campton. Jeff has two daughters, lives on a ski hill, and is close to one of Sharon's kids. Those kids now live in Vermont, New Hampshire, and Delaware.

Everyone has dogs and over the years some cats here and there. The Downs family had Teddy, the five-dollar beagle, for about fourteen years. She was a good dog. Suzie brought Mischu, a black coonhound, home for Jeff when she was in college. The dogs now have names such as Tilly, Fred, Marley, and Emma, and there's a cat named Ben.

All of the girls love to cook and sew and have given time to nonprofit groups and somehow find time to help others, to volunteer. The family was a doing and learning one.

"When we were first married, we decided that all the kids should have a college degree without debt, so we decided to pay for four years of college for each of them. We are also blessed that we've had no big accidents in the family and good health for us all."

The tragic part of this story was when their son-in-law, Doug, was diagnosed with a malignant brain tumor in March 1987. He died a week before Christmas that year when Sarah was eight months old, Cris, 2½, and Abbie, five. The families all loved him, and the love was sustained through caring and support for Sharon and her three children.

"We asked Sharon to move with us to New Hampshire right after Doug passed, but she needed to do things. So a year and half later, after Abbie's kindergarten year, late in 1988, Ray and Sharon figured out how to finish the lower level of their home in the White Mountains," said Elaine.

"We went to the local lumber store inquiring and buying cupboards, wallboard, whatever I needed," Ray said. "Jeff came over at one time to help, too, but then we decided we needed somebody professional. We ended up with a big L-shaped kitchen and hired someone to do the stuff I couldn't fix. The experienced house builder knew exactly how to do it. When the big L-shaped counter arrived, we helped juggle it in. We met Rick then, as he worked at the local lumber shop. We came in under budget, and Sharon and her children moved in 1989. She attended college, got her teaching certification and her master's, and decided to stay put, right here in the country of New Hampshire."

Sharon and Rick married a few years later and live in an old, beautiful home nearby in the woods.

"Very early in our marriage we assumed our roles, and it has been that way ever since. We take it for granted who is going to do what. If I need help in changing the beds, Ray will help out."

"And sometimes, I need Elaine's help when we need three or four hands. That seems to have worked well.

"We have never had any problem with money. If it was over a hundred dollars, we had to sleep on it. We never charged on credit more than what could be paid up that month. The only thing we ever bought on time was the clothes dryer. I don't really remember if we didn't have the money or why we did that. Mostly, if we didn't have the money, we didn't buy it. Anything except the house that is, and we had payments for that. We had three credit cards and always paid up the balance every month; we never had any interest accumulate—except one time. I was doing the income taxes and saw there was two dollars and fifty cents interest on one of the credit cards, which I thought I always paid ahead of the due date. I quizzed Elaine and thought it was she who hadn't paid up, but come to find out, it was me."

"We discussed everything," said Elaine. "Prior to marriage, we wanted a half dozen children and had four. We discussed money issues before we were married. When we went on a trip, Ray planned it but with what the kids or I wanted to see and do in mind. And when we returned, we both just dove in and unpacked together automatically.

"Patience works. Being lucky is nice, and we made the right choices the first time!"

Permanence is often used as a descriptor of Maine. I thought how apropos that was for Elaine and Ray, too. I feel a sense of permanence when I'm around them. Having known them for a few decades, I have never heard them utter anything negative to or about someone. There has always been a good way to say something, and it appears they have figured that out. They are two contented people who knew where they were going—together—a long time ago.

50 Years of Nice
Here's what they said.

This list contains strategies and traits of healthy, long-lasting marriages taken directly from the people interviewed for this book. And I could've plucked a few dozen more from their interviews, too! Just in case you missed it, here is the way it's done.

1. Don't give up.
2. Say "Don't worry" to your spouse when he or she is in a difficult situation.
3. Look at good examples of healthy marriages; be good examples.
4. Be hardworking, and select someone for a mate who is also hardworking.
5. Know what your duties are.
6. Establish your roles.
7. Husbands, be strong.
8. Wives, "cool it" verbally and maybe talk less.

9. Work together on just about everything that comes along.
10. Do what you have to do.
11. Have family functions.
12. If you don't have a sense of humor, develop one.
13. Communicate about everything.
14. Take on responsibilities.
15. Settle down.
16. Be complimentary.
17. Get help, counseling, or a third party if needed.
18. Do anything in the world for your spouse.
19. Be aware of the other's feelings.
20. Take good care of your children.
21. Go to church.
22. Follow through.
23. Do what you say you'll do.
24. Don't be selfish.
25. Teach morality to your family and, if needed, to yourself.
26. Accept your spouse's habits and faults.
27. Learn how to repair and figure out things yourselves.
28. Look to the future and plan economically.
29. Have the same family/couple goals.
30. Develop and have teamwork.
31. Become knowledgeable about money.
32. Check your ethics; pass them on.
33. Work on keeping your home up to par, salable, and in good condition.
34. Help others.
35. If possible, keep extended family attachments.
36. Entertain at home; find reasonable pastimes to fit time constraints, budget, and schedules.

37. Stay close to siblings and parents.
38. Know whom you account to.
39. Put pride aside.
40. Pray.
41. Analyze your economics; try to have Mom not work outside of the home during early child-raising years.
42. Think about what society demands and what influences you.
43. Redefine your responsibilities and roles occasionally; be open.
44. Be active in your church and your children's schools.
45. Have breakfast and dinner, or at least one meal, as a family.
46. Give each other some space.
47. Enjoy people; care for others.
48. Never be too busy to get together as a family; make it daily.
49. Education for many is important; pass it on to your children.
50. Don't think about changing your spouse…except maybe his socks.
51. Make sure your spouse can depend on you.
52. Try not to ever embarrass your spouse.
53. Don't hurt each other.
54. Make good choices about the people you are around; base your friend selections on their actions.
55. Treat your children as your jewels.
56. Don't be over demanding.
57. Check your money/financial needs, and give to the less fortunate.
58. Check your money/financial needs, and aim not to be needy yourselves.

59. Don't need "new stuff" all the time.
60. Remember and demonstrate that your spouse is the most important person in your life.
61. Honor your spouse; put your spouse and your children first.
62. Take on responsibilities, and trust that your spouse will do the same.
63. Discuss raising children and be on the same page.
64. Teach your children to respect their grandparents, elders, and others.
65. Know yourself.
66. Get involved when family problems arise; speak up if required, and help with solutions.
67. Don't avoid doing things when you'd rather avoid them; do them together.
68. Accept your spouse the way he/she is.
69. Bite your tongue.
70. Have fun together.
71. Keep in touch with friends.
72. Enjoy each other.
73. Learn how to compromise and use that skill when needed.
74. Try to be relaxed as an individual.
75. Always communicate: talk, talk, talk.
76. Level with one another.
77. Pull together.
78. Think about and remember what you liked and loved in your spouse in the first place.
79. Don't have too high or too many expectations of one another.
80. Work at your marriage, for your marriage.

81. Take vacations alone occasionally.
82. Don't argue over money.
83. Self-evaluate.
84. Remember, marriage is an everyday thing.
85. Have some common interests.
86. Hopefully, have same views on social issues, or at least talk, have an educated opinion, and respect your spouse's opinion.
87. Grow your marriage.
88. Act and be mature.
89. Tolerate a lot.
90. Remember, it is give and take.
91. Back up your spouse; try not to ask, "Why did you do that?"
92. It's good to have the same religion.
93. Trust your spouse.
94. Discuss and agree on child discipline before the baby comes.
95. Life is not to be lived just to analyze it.
96. You probably cannot change your spouse, so don't try.
97. Don't always do your own thing.
98. Marriage is work; face it and work.
99. Let your grown children work out their own problems.
100. Do some things on purpose.
101. Choose some pastimes, hobbies, or other interests that are good for the whole family.
102. Be happy around your own home.
103. Ask and let God guide you.
104. Be frugal when it matters to be frugal.
105. Be the right person; choose the right person in the first place.

106. Know that nothing is perfect.
107. Support your spouse in his/her interests.
108. Like each other.
109. Have patience.
110. Wait for each other.

Sources

Cherry Road School Project – Rootsweb

Ellsworth and the Statler Hotels – FreepagesAncestry.com

en.wikipedia.org/wiki/International_Harvester

en.wikipedia.org/wiki/Lynn_ Massachusetts

en.wikipedia.org/Seaford_NewYork

en.wikipedia.org/wiki/Statler_hotels

en.wikipedia.org/wiki/Young_Republicans

https://www.rit.edu/overview/history

Who Was Arthur Murray? Arthur Murray Dance Center

www.AdoptUSKids.org   Rhode Island Foster Care and
Adopting Guidelines

www.carrier.com   Willis Carrier – The inventor of mod-
ern air-conditioning

www.cemidatlantic.org/   Christian Endeavors - who we
are

www.deltamuseum.org/exhibits/delta -history

www.hibbing.mn.us/information: Tourism & History

www.massapequachamber.org/   About us

www.PanAmair.org/history

www.quantico.marines.mil/   About

www.sailcyc.com/   Canandaigua Yacht Club

Made in the USA
Middletown, DE
03 May 2015